전 세계 1,600만이 입증한

통문장 학습법

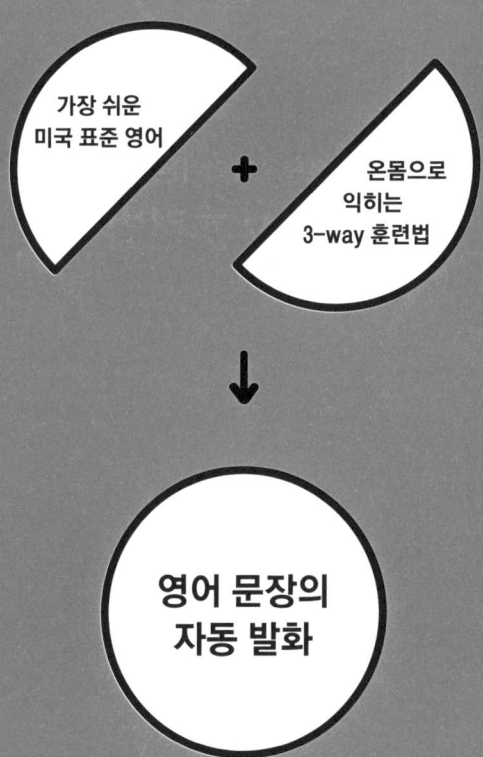

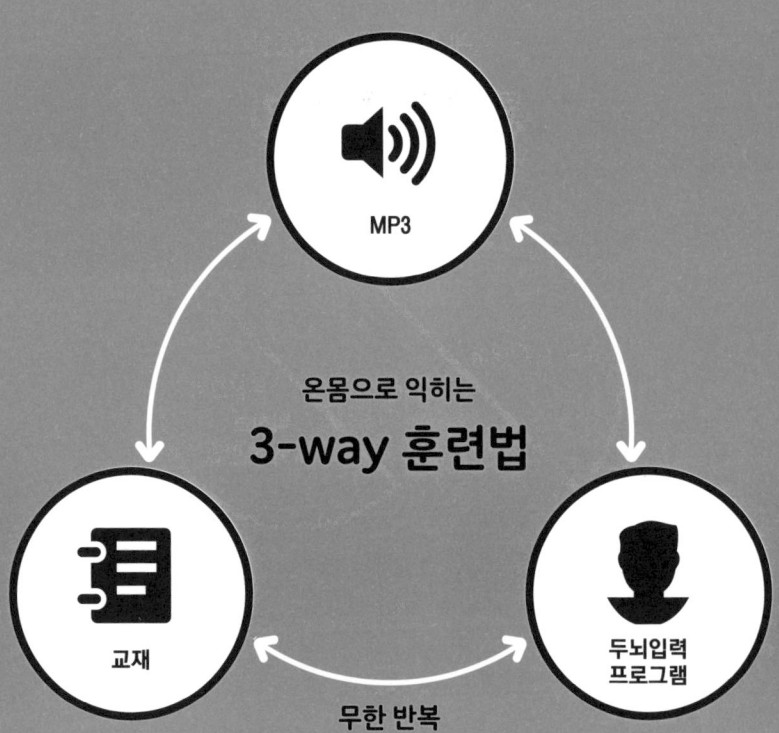

ENGLISH 900

3

Edwin T. Cornelius, Jr. 저

ENGLISH
900 전면개정판 ③

발행인	허문호
발행처	YBM
편집	정윤영
디자인	장선숙
삽화	이용택
마케팅	고영노, 김한석, 김동진, 박찬경, 문근호

초판발행 2017년 5월 8일
8쇄발행 2025년 8월 20일

신고일자 1964년 3월 28일
신고번호 제 1964-000003호
주소 서울시 종로구 종로 104
전화 (02) 2000-0515 [구입 문의] / (02) 2000-0463 [내용 문의]
팩스 (02) 2285-1523
홈페이지 www.ybmbooks.com

ISBN 978-89-17-22714-7

English 900
Original edition © 1971 by Edwin Cornelius, Jr.

All rights reserved.
English-Korean 1st edition © 2012 by Joanne Cornelius and YBM
English-Korean 2nd edition © 2017 by Joanne Cornelius and YBM

All rights reserved. No part of this publication may be reproduced, stored in a retrieval system, or transmitted in any form, or by any means, (electronic, mechanical, photocopying, recording or otherwise) without the prior written permission of both of the copyright owner and the publisher of this book.

이 책의 저작권은 저자에게 있으며, 책의 제호 및 디자인에 대한 모든 권리는 출판사인 YBM에게 있습니다.
서면에 의한 저자와 출판사의 허락 없이 내용의 일부 혹은 전부를 인용 및 복제하거나 발췌하는 것을 금합니다.
낙장 및 파본은 교환해 드립니다.
구입철회는 구매처 규정에 따라 교환 및 환불처리 됩니다.

어린아이처럼 배워라
그리고 반복하라!

영어 배우기에는 왕도가 없습니다. 자기 하기 나름입니다. 영어를 해야겠다는 마음이 얼마나 절실한지에 따라, 본인이 실제로 얼마나 노력하느냐에 따라 성과는 다르게 나타납니다. 하루 아침에 영어를 배우는 비법은 없습니다. 끊임없이 듣고 말하는 것이 제일 중요합니다.

예전에 아프리카 콩고에서 재미있는 연구를 했습니다. 영어를 한마디도 못하던 콩고 인이 3개월 만에 영어를 완벽히 구사하게 되었습니다. 말소리만 들으면 영락없이 영어 원어민이었지요. 요인은 무엇이었을까요. 바로 아프리카에 구전 전통이 있어서 가능했던 일입니다. 복잡하게 생각하지 않고, 무조건 말과 발음을 흉내내는 것이죠. 글로 읽거나 쓰며 익히는 게 아니라 듣고 따라하며 외우는 구전 전통이 말 익히기엔 최고라는 걸 여실히 보여준 거죠. 어린아이들이 언어를 익히는 것을 생각해보십시오. 어린아이처럼 배우십시오. 머뭇거리거나 실수를 두려워하면 영어를 배울 수 없습니다.

듣고 말하기의 실천법으로 제가 추천하는 방법은 '반복'입니다. 공부하는 내용을 완전히 자기 것으로 만들기 위해서는 '반복'이 필수이지요. 그래서 저는 수년간 듣고 말하기의 반복을 구현한 학습 교재 개발에 힘썼고 English 900 시리즈가 바로 그 결과물입니다. 이 교재를 가지고 듣고 말하는 데 주력하십시오. 학교 시절 배운 문법이나 어휘, 문장들 모두 다 여러분의 머릿속 어딘가에 있습니다. 이 교재는 여러 분들이 이미 배웠던 내용들이 듣고 말하기, 반복의 방식을 통해 다시 입 밖으로 나오도록 매우 효과적으로 도와줍니다. 말과 발음에 더욱 집중할 수 있도록 헤드폰을 끼고 열심히 듣고 따라 하십시오.

제가 혼신의 힘을 기울여 개발한 이 English 900 시리즈가
여러분의 영어 공부에
큰 힘이 되어드릴 것을 자신합니다.

Edwin T. Cornelius, Jr.

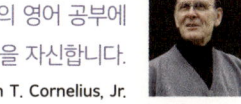

글로벌 베스트셀러
English 900

1963년 초판

2013년 한국어 개정판

2014년 일본어 개정판

2015년 중국어 개정판

언어학자 Cornelius가 미국 정부의 의뢰를 받아 만든 미국 표준 영어 교재

English 900은 전 세계에 미국 표준 영어를 보급하고자 미국 국무부가 미시간 대학에 의뢰하여 언어학자 Cornelius가 오랜 시간 연구하고 개발한 영어 교재입니다. 1970년대에는 대한민국 최초 오디오 교재로 출간되어 최다 판매를 기록하는 센세이션을 일으켰고, 전 세계적으로도 1,600만 부 이상 판매된 초대형 베스트셀러입니다.

English 900의 명성과 효과를 검증한 국내 개정판

English 900의 명성은 계속 그 대를 이어와 국내 독자들의 재출간 요청이 꾸준히 있었습니다. 2013년 드디어 대한민국 대표 영어 강사 이보영, 아이작 선생님의 친절하고 자세한 해설강의로 한층 업그레이드된 한국어 개정판 New English 900이 출간되었고, 2016년까지 총 22만 부가 판매되어 다시금 그 명성과 학습효과를 입증했습니다.

일본 열도와 중국 대륙까지 점령한 English 900 열풍

English 900의 재출간을 열망한 것은 대한민국의 학습자뿐만이 아니었습니다. 2014년 일본 아사히 프레스, 2015년 중국 금일금중 출판사도 개정판 출간의 대열에 합류하여 2,30대 젊은 영어 학습자들에게 좋은 반응을 얻고 있습니다.

2017년 한국어 전면개정판
무엇이 업그레이드되었나?

2017년 한국어 전면개정판

1. 오리지널 English 900의 정통성과 장점은 그대로 살렸습니다!

희미한 옛 기억 속 중학교 영어 교과서에서 본 듯한 익숙한 문장들---일상생활에서 실제로 쓰이는 실용적이고 매우 쉬운 문장들만으로도 얼마든지 의사소통이 자유롭다는 Cornelius 박사의 믿음을 전면개정판에서도 그대로 이어가고 있습니다.

2. 지금 세대의 일상 주제와 그들이 말하는 표준영어를 담았습니다!

전 세계의 문화는 급변했고 현 세대의 언어생활 또한 실용성을 추구하는 방향으로 변화하고 있습니다. 따라서 전면개정판에서는 교재의 문장과 대화문을 통해 다루고 있는 일상의 장면들 중 현 세대와 맞지 않는 일부 주제 및 문장들을 지금의 영어권 사람들이 말하는 영어로 교체했습니다.

3. 통문장학습법의 실천법까지 제공해드립니다!

전면개정판에서는 '학습해야 할 것(what to learn)'뿐만 아니라 '학습하는 방법(how to learn)'을 함께 제시합니다. 통문장 두뇌 입력 프로그램, 다양한 형식의 훈련용 MP3 파일이 통문장학습의 든든한 조력자가 될 것입니다.

English 900으로 이룬
5분의 작은 기적

2016년 여름 경북매일신문의 "전교생 48명, 포항 시골 장기초교 '5분의 작은 기적'"이라는 제목의 기사를 통해 New English 900 교재를 활용하여 영어공부를 하는 초등학생들과 교사들이 소개된 바 있습니다. English 900 온라인 카페의 성실멤버이기도 한 이 학교의 교장, 이성규 선생님을 만나보았습니다.

'5분의 작은 기적' 이란?

이성규 교장선생님 다른 행사 취재차 학교를 방문했던 기자가 우연히 우리 학교의 5분 영어 프로그램 설명을 듣고 감명을 받아 직접 교실을 방문하고 취재하여 '5분의 작은 기적'이라는 제목으로 신문에 소개한 것이죠. New English 900 초급 교재를 활용하여 제가 직접 개발한 컴퓨터 프로그램으로 매일 1교시 수업 전에 5분간 선생님들이 지도한 결과 학생들이 게임만 하던 컴퓨터로 영어 공부를 하고, 평가 프로그램으로 스스로 평가하고, 선생님께 상도 받으면서 즐겁게 공부를 하게 되었습니다.

English 900을 교재로 택하신 이유는?

이성규 교장선생님 English 900은 학생 시절 다 마스터하지 못했다가 2013년에 새롭게 출시된 New English 900으로 다시 공부를 시작한 것이지요. 900개 기본 문장을 지금 11번째 복습 중인데, 이 교재의 좋은 점은 900이라는 뚜렷한 목표점을 가지고 공부할 수 있다는 것이지요. 학교에서 사용하는 영어 교과서도 좋지만 세계적으로 검증된 교재를 가지고 아이들이 초급회화 300문장이라는 목표에 우선적으로 도전하게 하면, 졸업 후까지도 계속 연결하여 공부할 수 있겠다는 생각으로 이 교재를 선택했습니다.

이성규 교장선생님 1권에 수록되어 있는 초급회화 300문장은 교과서에 나오는 문장도 많이 있어서 고학년에서는 300문장을 모두 마스터한 아이도 있습니다. 1학년부터 6학년까지 전교생이 100개까지는 거의 마스터했으니 계속 지도한다면 가능하다고 생각됩니다. 교사가 직접 모든 내용을 가르치기보다는 학생들이 스스로 공부할 수 있는 마인드를 키워주니 무리 없이 잘 따라오고 있습니다.

어른들 교재인데 아이들에게 어렵지 않았나?

900개 통문장이 정말 효과가 있었나?

이성규 교장선생님 English 900은 말하기 위주의 학습에 더 효과적이라고 생각합니다. 저도 듣기는 약하지만 이제 말하기는 어느 정도 자신이 있습니다. 이 책의 900개 기본 문장은 우리말만 봐도 거의 0.5초 내에 영어 문장이 나옵니다. 물론 900 문장만 외운다고 해서 말하기가 완벽히 된다고 할 수는 없지만 다른 표현까지 응용하여 말할 수 있는 기본 실력을 갖추게 된다고 생각합니다.

이성규 교장선생님 학습한 횟수도 중요하지만 내가 학습한 내용을 얼마나 알고 있는지 확인해보는 것이 중요하다고 생각합니다. 종이에 쓰면서 확인해도 좋지만, 우리의 궁극적인 목표가 '말하기'이니 영어로 직접 말해보고 음원으로 바로 정답을 확인하면 더욱 효과적일 것 같아서 개발한 프로그램이 '자율평가 프로그램'입니다. 학습한 내용을 스스로 평가하여 확인하면 더욱 동기 부여가 되겠지요. 또 정기적으로 원어민과 대화할 수 있는 기회를 마련하여 학습한 내용을 활용하는 것도 중요합니다.

다른 학습자들에게 전수하고픈 노하우는?

English 900으로
이런 효과 보았다!

영어회화 학습자의 마지막 선택

저도 영어회화에 한(?)이 맺혀서 정말 수많은 방법론에 매달려 많은 시간을 보냈어요. 그러다가 찾아낸 보물 같은 영어회화 교재가 English 900이었죠. 이 책의 최대 강점은 영어회화의 목표와 분량이 확실하다는 것입니다. 제가 공부한 경험으로는 900개의 문장은 아주 적당한 분량이며 수준도 어렵지 않아요. 이 교재로 반복해서 우리말을 듣고 영어로 말하는 훈련을 하다 보면, 하고 싶은 우리말이 떠오르는 순간 영어가 입에서 자동으로 튀어나오는 놀라운 경험을 하게 될 것입니다.

31만 방문 블로그 '영어백편의자현' 운영자, 김동건

영어 말하기 연습을 위한 최고의 교재

English 900은 제가 대학을 다닐 때 선풍적인 인기를 끌었던 영어회화 교재였어요. 아마 지금 40대 이상의 부모님들에게는 매우 친숙한 이름이 아닐까 싶습니다. 영어교사를 준비하던 저는 900개의 기본 문장들과 거기에서 파생된 문장들을 외워가며 English 900과 씨름을 했어요. 책이 점점 낡아가는 정도와 비례해 영어회화에 대한 자신감은 커져갔고, 간혹 만나는 외국인들 앞에서 하고 싶은 말들이 튀어나올 때 그 신기함과 희열은 이루 말할 수가 없었습니다.

차준식 영어교실 운영자, 고등학교 영어교사, 차준식

저 보고 English 900전도사래요

2년 전 이 책을 만나 그 효과를 실감한 저는 그 후 1년간 주변의 많은 사람들에게 이 책을 권하지 않을 수 없었죠. 저에게 소개 받은 분들이 또 다른 분들에게 추천하는 식으로 그렇게 김해의 많은 분들이 이 책을 공부하게 되었어요. 도서관에서 이 책에 관심을 보이는 사람들끼리 스터디 모임도 결성해 주 1회 함께 공부도 했는데, 작년에는 이 책으로 저와 함께 1년간 공부한 50대 지인의 영어 실력이 눈에 띄게 향상되고 자신 있게 해외 자유여행도 다녀오셨다고 하여 보람을 느꼈답니다. 새로 개정되는 책도 영어를 공부하는 많은 이들에게 등불 같은 존재가 되길 기원해봅니다.

초등학교 방과후 영어강사, 장은주

직장인이 되어 사무 현장에서 영어 쓸 일을 직접 겪다 보니, 영어를 잘하고 싶다는 마음이 학교 다닐 때보다 더 간절하게 듭니다. 영어 잘하는 직장 선배에게 조언을 구하니 무조건 말하고 외우는 게 정석이라고 하네요. New English 900에 반영된 코넬리우스의 영어회화 학습법이 딱 맞을 것 같더군요. 공부해보니 역시나 이만한 학습법은 없는 것 같습니다. 반복해서 말하고 트레이닝하다 보니 어느새 표현이 입에 착착 붙네요.

> 영어회화 학습의 정석이네요

28세, 직장인, 이희원

> 강사도 추천하는 교재입니다

English 900에는 실생활에서 쓰이는 어렵지 않은 영어 문장 900개가 들어 있어, 혼자서도 쉽게 공부할 수 있는 교재입니다. 예전부터 이 교재에 대해 알고 있어서, 주변에서 쉬운 영어 교재를 추천해달라고 할 때마다 주저 없이 권했습니다.

35세, 영어강사, 최지웅

900개 문장만 공부하면 영어가 된다고 해서 이게 무슨 말인가 했어요. 한편으로는 900개면 너무 많은 거 아닌가 생각도 했었는데, 막상 책을 보고 하루에 하라는 만큼만 하니 부담스럽지 않던데요. 혼자 영어 공부하기 부담되시는 분들에게 적절한 교재 같아요.

> 부담 없어요

23세, 대학생, 원미향

> 쉬운 단어로 이루어진 문장이 좋아요

직장을 관두고 영어와는 담을 쌓고 지내왔는데 영어를 더 멀리하면 안 되겠다는 생각에 English 900을 공부했습니다. 책에서 제시하는 대로 계속 반복해서 듣고 말하니 나중에는 진짜 영어 문장을 보지 않아도 입에서 문장이 나오네요. 어려운 단어를 사용하지 않아도 영어로 말할 수 있다는 걸 이번에 처음 알았습니다.

32세, 전업주부, 황미경

English 900 사용설명서

4단계 학습으로
기본 문장 300개 반복 훈련

 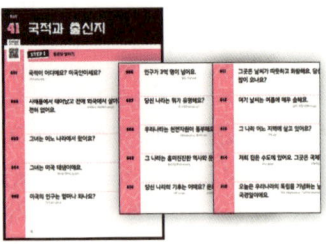

STEP 1 통문장 말하기

기본 문장을 5개씩 먼저 우리말로 보고 영어로 말해보세요. 말이 되든 안 되든 직접 말해보세요.

 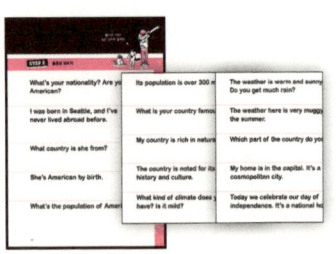

STEP 2 통문장 외우기

왼쪽 페이지에서 우리말을 보고 스스로 말해본 것을 이제 확인하며 암기하세요. 큰 소리로 2회 읽으세요.

 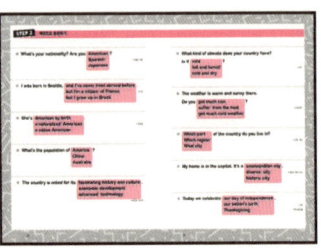

STEP 3 패턴으로 훈련하기

패턴 형태로 앞에서 배운 기본 문장을 한번 더 반복하여 암기 효과뿐 아니라 응용할 수 있는 역량까지 기르세요.

 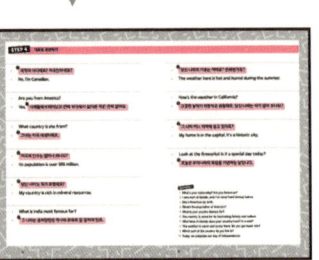

STEP 4 대화로 훈련하기

의사소통의 핵심은 대화죠. 대화의 기본 형태인 묻고 답하기 방식으로 기본 문장의 쓰임을 익히세요.

다양한 MP3 파일로
300문장 귀에 새기기!

통문장 말하기
우리말 문장 듣기 → 스스로 영어로 말해보기 → 영어 문장 듣고 확인하기

통문장 외우기
우리말 문장 듣기 → 영어 문장 2회 따라 말하기

패턴으로 훈련하기
영어 문장 1회 따라 말하기

대화로 훈련하기
영어 문장 1회 따라 말하기

통문장 영어만 듣기
출퇴근길, 소리 내어 훈련할 수 없을 때 기본 문장만 영어로 빠르게 듣기

총 5가지 종류의 MP3 파일을 활용하여
300문장의 암기 효과를 높여보세요!

English 900 사용설명서

통문장 두뇌입력 프로그램으로 300문장 뇌에 새기기!

통문장 두뇌입력 프로그램 이란?

2단계 구성을 통해 통문장을 눈으로 보고, 귀로 듣고, 입으로 말하며 반복 훈련하는 트레이닝용 동영상이예요.

1단계 청크 단위 암기 훈련

STEP 1
청크 단위 암기 훈련
"문장을 덩어리씩 늘려가며 큰소리로 따라 말해봅시다!"

처음부터 문장 전체를 외우는 게 부담스럽다면 문장을 덩어리씩 늘려가며 훈련하면 단기간에 통문장 학습에 적응할 수 있어요.

2단계 자동 발화 훈련

STEP 2
자동 발화 훈련
"우리말 문장을 영어로 말해본 후, 들려주는 영어 문장을 2회 따라 합시다!"

1단계에서 누적 학습한 효과로 통문장이 입에서 자동으로 나오는 것을 확인하며 말하기에 대한 자심감을 얻는 단계예요.

이런 좋은 프로그램을 어디서 만날 수 있죠?

각 Day의 첫 페이지에 있는 QR 코드를 휴대폰으로 찍으면 바로 재생하여 편리하게 학습할 수 있어요.

두뇌입력 프로그램 활용을 위한
QR 코드 이용법

QR 코드가 있는
각 Day 시작 페이지를
펼쳐보세요.

네이버 어플리케이션을
실행하여 QR 코드를
읽어 보세요.

검색창 옆에 마이크 모양을 누르세요.

여러 아이콘들 중 QR 코드 모양을
누르세요.

카메라 화면이 나오면 교재의
QR 코드를 읽을 수 있게 가까
이 대주세요.

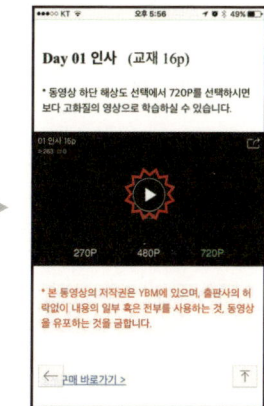

QR 코드가 제대로 읽히면 두뇌입력
프로그램으로 바로 연결됩니다. 세모
모양의 버튼을 누르면 재생됩니다.

* 네이버 어플리케이션 외에도 QR 코드를 읽어주는 여러 어플리케이션이 있습니다. 구글 플레이스토어 또는 아이폰 앱스토어에서 "QR코드 리더"로 검색하셔서 관련 어플리케이션을 설치해 사용하셔도 됩니다.

English 900 ❸ 목차

> 프리토킹 통문장 300개

Day 41	국적과 출신지	16
Day 42	직업과 경력	26
Day 43	학력과 학업	36
Day 44	취향과 기호	46
Day 45	취미와 관심사	56
Day 46	스포츠 활동	66
Day 47	음악 활동과 독서	76
Day 48	TV 시청	86
Day 49	뉴스와 미디어	96
Day 50	글로벌 이슈	106

Day 51	에피소드 말하기 1	116
Day 52	에피소드 말하기 2	126
Day 53	앞으로의 일 가정하기	136
Day 54	과거에 대한 아쉬움과 후회	146
Day 55	정중한 부탁과 요청	156
Day 56	회의와 발표	166
Day 57	의견 묻고 답하기	176
Day 58	다양한 의견에 대응하기	186
Day 59	조언과 충고	196
Day 60	의사 결정	206

ENGLISH 900 ①
기초회화 통문장
300개

ENGLISH 900 ②
일상회화 통문장
300개

41 국적과 출신지

STEP 1 통문장 말하기

601 국적이 어디예요? 미국인이세요?
국적 nationality

602 시애틀에서 태어났고 전에 외국에서 살아본 적은 전혀 없어요.
외국에서, 해외에서 abroad

603 그녀는 어느 나라에서 왔어요?

604 그녀는 미국 태생이에요.
태어날 때부터 by birth

605 미국의 인구는 얼마나 되나요?
인구 population

STEP 2 통문장 외우기

What's your nationality? Are you American?

I was born in Seattle, and I've never lived abroad before.

What country is she from?

She's American by birth.

What's the population of America?

STEP 1 통문장 말하기

606 인구가 3억 명이 넘어요.
넘는, 이상 over

607 당신 나라는 뭐가 유명해요?
~로 유명한 famous for

608 우리나라는 천연자원이 풍부해요.
자원 resources 풍부한 rich

609 그 나라는 흥미진진한 역사와 문화로 잘 알려져 있죠.
흥미진진한 fascinating   ~로 유명하다 be noted for

610 당신 나라의 기후는 어때요? 온화한가요?
기후 climate   온화한, 포근한 mild

STEP 2 통문장 외우기

Its population is over 300 million.

What is your country famous for?

My country is rich in natural resources.

The country is noted for its fascinating history and culture.

What kind of climate does your country have? Is it mild?

STEP 1 통문장 말하기

611 그곳은 날씨가 따뜻하고 화창해요. 당신 나라는 비가 많이 오나요?

612 여기 날씨는 여름에 매우 습해요.
습한, 후텁지근한 muggy

613 그 나라 어느 지역에 살고 있어요?
지역 part

614 저희 집은 수도에 있어요. 그곳은 국제적인 도시예요.
수도 capital   국제적인, 세계적인 cosmopolitan

615 오늘은 우리나라의 독립을 기념하는 날입니다. 국경일이에요.
독립 independence 기념하다 celebrate

STEP 2 통문장 외우기

The weather is warm and sunny there. Do you get much rain?

The weather here is very muggy during the summer.

Which part of the country do you live in?

My home is in the capital. It's a cosmopolitan city.

Today we celebrate our day of independence. It's a national holiday.

STEP 3 패턴으로 훈련하기

❶ What's your nationality? Are you American ?
　　　　　　　　　　　　　　　　　Spanish*
　　　　　　　　　　　　　　　　　Japanese

*스페인 사람

❷ I was born in Seattle, and I've never lived abroad before .
　　　　　　　　　　　　but I'm a citizen* of France
　　　　　　　　　　　　but I grew up in Brazil

*시민

❸ She's American by birth .
　　　　 a naturalized* American
　　　　 a native American

*귀화한

❹ What's the population of America ?
　　　　　　　　　　　　　 China
　　　　　　　　　　　　　 Australia

❺ The country is noted for its fascinating history and culture .
　　　　　　　　　　　　　　　economic development
　　　　　　　　　　　　　　　advanced* technology

*선진의, 첨단의

⑥ What kind of climate does your country have?

Is it mild ?
hot and humid*
cold and dry

*습한

⑦ The weather is warm and sunny there.

Do you get much rain ?
suffer* from the heat
get much cold weather

*시달리다

⑧ Which part of the country do you live in?
Which region*
What city

*지역, 지방

⑨ My home is in the capital. It's a cosmopolitan city .
diverse* city
historic city

*다양한 면이 있는

⑩ Today we celebrate our day of independence .
our nation's birth*
Thanksgiving*

*건국
*추수감사절

STEP 4 대화로 훈련하기

A **국적이 어디예요? 미국인이세요?**
B No, I'm Canadian.

A Are you from America?
B Yes, **시애틀에서 태어났고 전에 외국에서 살아본 적은 전혀 없어요.**

A What country is she from?
B **그녀는 미국 태생이에요.**

A **미국의 인구는 얼마나 되나요?**
B Its population is over 300 million.

A **당신 나라는 뭐가 유명해요?**
B My country is rich in mineral resources.

A What is India most famous for?
B **그 나라는 흥미진진한 역사와 문화로 잘 알려져 있죠.**

A 당신 나라의 기후는 어때요? 온화한가요?
B The weather here is hot and humid during the summer.

A How's the weather in California?
B 그곳은 날씨가 따뜻하고 화창해요. 당신 나라는 비가 많이 오나요?

A 그 나라 어느 지역에 살고 있어요?
B My home is in the capital. It's a historic city.

A Look at the fireworks! Is it a special day today?
B 오늘은 우리나라의 독립을 기념하는 날입니다.

ANSWERS!!

1. What's your nationality? Are you American?
2. I was born in Seattle, and I've never lived abroad before.
3. She's American by birth.
4. What's the population of America?
5. What is your country famous for?
6. The country is noted for its fascinating history and culture.
7. What kind of climate does your country have? Is it mild?
8. The weather is warm and sunny there. Do you get much rain?
9. Which part of the country do you live in?
10. Today we celebrate our day of independence.

42 직업과 경력

STEP 1 통문장 말하기

616 어떤 일을 하세요? 영업 사원이세요?
영업 사원, 판매원 salesperson

617 영어 교사예요. 그린우드 고등학교에서 가르쳐요.

618 교육을 마치는 대로 은행원이 될 거예요.
~하자마자 as soon as

619 제 사업을 키웠어요. 작은 식당을 소유하고 있어요.
발전시키다 build up   소유하다 own

620 아버지는 민간 항공기 조종사였어요. 얼마 전에
민간의 commercial   조종사 pilot
은퇴하셨죠.
은퇴하다 retire

STEP 2 통문장 외우기

What kind of work do you do? Are you a salesperson?

I'm an English teacher. I teach at Greenwood High School.

As soon as I complete my training, I'm going to be a bank teller.

I have built up my own business. I own a small restaurant.

My father was a commercial pilot. He just retired.

STEP 1　통문장 말하기

621 삼촌은 정치인이에요. 그는 주지사 선거에 출마 중이죠.
정치인 politician　　주지사 governor　　~에 입후보하다 run for

622 그는 사업에서 성공적인 경력을 쌓은 뒤 대사로 임명되었어요.
경력 career　　대사 ambassador
임명하다 appoint

623 형은 군대에 있는데 내년 3월에 제대할 거예요.
입대 중인 be in the army　　제대하다 be discharged

624 헬렌은 결혼하기 전에 비서로 일했어요.
비서 secretary

625 그녀의 남편은 변호사예요. 개인 사무실을 갖고 있어요.
(전문직 종사자의) 개인 사무실 one's own practice

STEP 2 통문장 외우기

My uncle is a politician. He's running for governor.

After a successful career in business, he was appointed as an ambassador.

My brother's in the army and he will be discharged next March.

Helen worked as a secretary before she got married.

Her husband is a lawyer. He has his own practice.

STEP 1　통문장 말하기

626 그는 늘 자신의 일에 자부심을 갖고 있어요. 매우 유능하죠.
~에 자부심을 가지다 take pride in
유능한 efficient

627 졸업하면 뭘 하고 싶어요? 생각해본 적 있어요?
졸업하다 graduate

628 의료 업계에 종사하는 걸 생각해본 적이 있나요?
의료, 의술 medicine

629 근무 시간이 좋은 고소득 직업을 갖고 싶어요.
보수를 많이 주는 well-paid

630 그림 그리는 걸 좋아하지만 그걸 평생 직업으로 삼고 싶진 않아요.

STEP 2 통문장 외우기

He always takes pride in his work. He's very efficient.

What do you want to do after you graduate? Have you thought about it?

Have you ever thought about a career in medicine?

I'd like to have a well-paid job with excellent hours.

I like painting, but I wouldn't want it to be my life's work.

STEP 3 패턴으로 훈련하기

❶ What kind of work do you do? Are you a | salesperson / government officer / secretary | ?

❷ As soon as I complete my training, I'm going to be a | bank teller / pilot / hotel manager | .

❸ I have built up my own business. I | own a small restaurant / have a taxi company / run a beauty salon* | .

*미용실

❹ My father was a | commercial pilot / police officer* / professor* | . He just retired.

*경찰관
*교수

❺ My uncle is a politician. He's running for | governor / mayor* / congress* | .

*시장(市長)
*의회, 국회

❻ Helen worked as [a secretary / an office worker / a flight attendant*] before she got married.

*승무원

❼ Her husband is [a lawyer / a doctor / an accountant]. He has his own practice.

❽ He always takes pride in his work. He's very [efficient / meticulous* / dedicated*].

*꼼꼼한
*헌신적인

❾ What do you want to do [after you graduate / when you finish your training / after you finish school]?

❿ I'd like to have a well-paid job with [excellent hours / good working conditions / a lot of benefits*].

*복지 혜택

STEP 4 　 대화로 훈련하기

A　❶ 어떤 일을 하세요? 영업 사원이세요?

B　No, I'm a government officer.

A　What's your plan after graduation?

B　❷ 교육을 마치는 대로 은행원이 될 거예요.

A　What do you do? Are you an office worker?

B　❸ 제 사업을 키웠어요. 작은 식당을 소유하고 있어요.

A　Does your father still work?

B　❹ 아버지는 민간 항공기 조종사였어요. 얼마 전에 은퇴하셨죠.

A　❺ 삼촌은 정치인이에요. 그는 주지사 선거에 출마 중이죠.

B　That's why he looked so familiar.

A　I haven't seen your brother lately. How's he doing?

B　❻ 형은 군대에 있는데 내년 3월에 제대할 거예요.

A I know your brother-in-law works for a big law firm.
B Yes, ❼ 그는 늘 자신의 일에 자부심을 갖고 있어요. 매우 유능하죠.

A ❽ 졸업하면 뭘 하고 싶어요? 생각해본 적 있어요?
B I'd like to have a well-paid job with excellent hours.

A ❾ 의료 업계에 종사하는 걸 생각해본 적이 있나요?
B Never. I hate going to the doctor even when I'm sick.

A I think you are really good at painting. Why don't you go to art school?
B ❿ 그림 그리는 걸 좋아하지만 그걸 평생 직업으로 삼고 싶진 않아요.

ANSWERS!!

1 What kind of work do you do? Are you a salesperson?
2 As soon as I complete my training, I'm going to be a bank teller.
3 I have built up my own business. I own a small restaurant.
4 My father was a commercial pilot. He just retired.
5 My uncle is a politician. He's running for governor.
6 My brother's in the army and he will be discharged next March.
7 he always takes pride in his work. He's very efficient.
8 What do you want to do after you graduate? Have you thought about it?
9 Have you ever thought about a career in medicine?
10 I like painting, but I wouldn't want it to be my life's work.

43 학력과 학업

STEP 1 통문장 말하기

631 뉴욕에서 초등학교를, 그리고 시카고에서 고등학교를 다녔어요.
초등학교 grade school(= elementary school)

632 초등학교에서 숫자 계산하는 걸 배웠어요.

633 중학교에서 한국사에 대해 배웠어요.

634 지금 대학 몇 학년이에요?
학년 year

635 올해가 대학에서의 첫해예요. 1학년이에요.
1학년 freshman

STEP 2   통문장 외우기

I went to grade school in New York, and high school in Chicago.

In elementary school, I learned to calculate numbers.

I learned about Korean history in middle school.

What year are you in college right now?

This is my first year of college. I'm a freshman.

STEP 1 통문장 말하기

636 컬럼비아 대학 졸업생이에요.
졸업생 graduate

637 대학에서 경제학을 전공했어요. 당신의 전공은 뭐였어요?
경제학 economics   ~을 전공하다 major in   전공 major

638 영어 교육 학사 학위가 있어요.
학사 학위 bachelor's degree

639 여동생은 막 고등학교를 졸업했어요.
~를 졸업하다 graduate from

640 형은 교수예요. 문학을 가르쳐요.
교수진 faculty   문학 literature

STEP 2 통문장 외우기

I'm a graduate of Columbia University.

In college, I majored in economics. What was your major?

I have a bachelor's degree in English Education.

My younger sister just graduated from high school.

My older brother is a member of the faculty. He teaches literature.

STEP 1 통문장 말하기

641 대학 다니는 동안 기숙사에서 지냈나요?
기숙사 dormitory

642 비용이 더 들긴 하지만 캠퍼스 밖에 있는 아파트를 임대했어요.
캠퍼스 밖의 off-campus

643 틀림없이 대학 때 높은 성적을 받았을 것 같아요.
성적 grade

644 대학 첫해에 전 과목 A학점을 받았어요.
연속적인 straight

645 학과 외 활동에 참여하느라 좋은 학점을 못 받았어요.
학과 외의 extracurricular   ~에 참여하다 participate in

STEP 2 통문장 외우기

Did you live in a dormitory during college?

I rented an off-campus apartment though it cost more.

I'm sure you received high grades in college.

During my first year of college, I made straight As.

I participated in extracurricular activities, so I couldn't get good grades.

STEP 3 패턴으로 훈련하기

❶ In elementary school, I learned to | calculate numbers / read and write / pronounce* letters |.

*발음하다

❷ I | learned about Korean history / studied physics* and chemistry* / took a physical education* class | in middle school.

*물리학 / *화학
*체육

❸ What year | are you / is your sister / is your son | in | college / high school / elementary school | right now?

❹ This is my | first / second / third / fourth | year of college. I'm a | freshman / sophomore* / junior* / senior* |.

*2학년
*3학년
*4학년

❺ I'm a graduate of | Columbia University / Harvard Business School* / MIT* |.

*하버드 경영 대학원
*매사추세츠 공과 대학

⑥ In college, I majored in | economics | . What was your major?
| linguistics* | *언어학
| philosophy* | *철학

⑦ I have a | bachelor's | degree in English Education.
| master's* | *석사의
| doctorate* | *박사의

⑧ My younger sister just graduated from | high school | .
| college |
| medical school |

⑨ My older brother is a member of the faculty.
He teaches | literature | .
| economics |
| psychology* | *심리학

⑩ During my first year of college, I made | straight As | .
| good grades |
| a B average |

43

STEP 4 대화로 훈련하기

A Have you studied in America?
B Yes, ① 뉴욕에서 초등학교를, 그리고 시카고에서 고등학교를 다녔어요.

A When did you learn about Korean history?
B ② 중학교에서 한국사에 대해 배웠어요.

A ③ 지금 대학 몇 학년이에요?
B This is my second year of college. I'm a sophomore.

A What college did you go to?
B ④ 컬럼비아 대학 졸업생이에요.

A ⑤ 대학에서 경제학을 전공했어요. 당신의 전공은 뭐였나요?
B I have a bachelor's degree in linguistics.

A What was your major in college?
B ⑥ 영어 교육 학사 학위가 있어요.

A Are your brothers and sisters all college graduates?
B Not yet. ⑦ 여동생은 막 고등학교를 졸업했어요.

A ⑧ 대학 다니는 동안 기숙사에서 지냈나요?
B No, I rented an off-campus apartment though it cost more.

A ⑨ 틀림없이 대학 때 높은 성적을 받았을 것 같아요.
B I participated in extracurricular activities, so I couldn't get good grades.

A ⑩ 대학 첫해에 전 과목 A학점을 받았어요.
B Well, I never even made a B until I was a senior.

ANSWERS!!

1 I went to grade school in New York, and high school in Chicago.
2 I learned about Korean history in middle school.
3 What year are you in college right now?
4 I'm a graduate of Columbia University.
5 In college, I majored in economics. What was your major?
6 I have a bachelor's degree in English Education.
7 My younger sister just graduated from high school.
8 Did you live in a dormitory during college?
9 I'm sure you received high grades in college.
10 During my first year of college, I made straight As.

44 취향과 기호

STEP 1 통문장 말하기

646 지하철을 못 견디겠어요.
견디다 stand

647 지하철의 어떤 점이 마음에 들지 않는 거죠?

648 지하철이 정말 붐빌 때 마음에 들지 않아요.
(사람들이) 붐비는 crowded

649 이 도시에 대해 마음에 들지 않는 한 가지는 도로에 늘 차가 너무 많다는 거예요.

650 시금치가 몸에 좋다는 건 알지만 좋아하지 않아요.
시금치 spinach   비록 ~지만 even though

STEP 2 통문장 외우기

I can't stand the subway.

What is it that you don't like about the subway?

I don't like it when the subway gets really crowded.

One thing I don't like about this city is that there are always too many cars on the road.

I don't like spinach even though I know it's good for me.

STEP 1 통문장 말하기

651 당신은 음식에 대해 좀 지나치게 까다로운 것 같아요.
까다로운 picky

652 그 주스 맛은 별로였지만 어쨌든 마셨어요.
맛 taste

653 그를 왜 그렇게 많이 싫어해요?

654 그는 모든 것에서 흠을 잡아내요.
~의 흠을 잡다 find fault with

655 그는 제가 하는 행동이나 말은 뭐든지 안 좋아해요.

STEP 2 통문장 외우기

I'm afraid you're a little too picky about food.

I didn't like the taste of the juice, but I drank it anyway.

Why do you dislike him so much?

He finds fault with everything.

He doesn't like anything I do or say.

STEP 1 통문장 말하기

656 그는 간섭 받는 걸 싫어해요.
통제하다, 지배하다 control

657 가장 좋아하는 취미 활동이 뭐예요?
취미, 재미로 하는 것 pastime

658 테니스 치는 걸 좋아하지만 아주 잘하진 못해요.

659 영화에 대한 안목이 훌륭하네요.
안목, 감식력 taste

660 그 영화에서 뭐가 가장 좋았어요?

STEP 2 통문장 외우기

He doesn't like the idea of being controlled.

What's your favorite pastime?

I like to play tennis, but I'm not a very good player.

You have wonderful taste in movies.

What did you like best about the movie?

STEP 3　패턴으로 훈련하기

❶ I can't stand / can't deal with* / really hate* the subway.

*대하다, 다루다
*싫어하다

❷ What is it that you don't like / hate / like so much about the subway?

❸ I don't like it when the subway gets really / unusually* / terribly crowded.

*대단히, 몹시

❹ I don't like spinach even though I know it's good for me / it makes me healthy* / I have to eat it.

*건강한

❺ I'm afraid you're a little too picky / particular* / fussy* about food.

*까다로운
*까다로운

❻ He | finds fault with | everything.
     | sees the negative* side of |
     | is critical* of |

*부정적인
*비판적인, 비난하는

❼ He doesn't | like | anything I do or say.
            | care for* |
            | pay attention to* |

*~을 (아주) 좋아하다
*~에 주목하다

❽ What's your favorite | pastime | ?
                       | hobby* |
                       | game |

*취미

❾ I like to play | tennis | but I'm not a very good player.
                 | table tennis* |
                 | golf |

*탁구

❿ What did you like best about the | movie | ?
                                    | book |
                                    | play |

STEP 4 대화로 훈련하기

A ① 지하철을 못 견디겠어요.
B Neither can I. Hey, let's take a taxi.

A What is it that you don't like about the subway?
B ② 지하철이 정말 붐빌 때 마음에 들지 않아요.

A What made you decide to leave here?
B ③ 이 도시에 대해 마음에 들지 않는 한 가지는 도로에 늘 차가 너무 많다는 거예요.

A Don't take the spinach out of your pasta. You're just like a kid.
B ④ 시금치가 몸에 좋다는 건 알지만 좋아하지 않아요.

A ⑤ 당신은 음식에 대해 좀 지나치게 까다로운 것 같아요.
B I am not a picky eater at all. It just tastes so bad.

A ⑥ 그를 왜 그렇게 많이 싫어해요?
B He finds fault with everything.

A　Why does he always get mad at his parents?
B　❼ 그는 간섭 받는 걸 싫어해요.

A　❽ 가장 좋아하는 취미 활동이 뭐예요?
B　I love watching TV and playing chess.

A　Can you teach me how to play tennis?
B　Well, ❾ 테니스 치는 걸 좋아하지만 아주 잘하진 못해요.

A　❿ 영화에 대한 안목이 훌륭하네요.
B　Thanks, but I watch movies just for fun.

ANSWERS!!

1　I can't stand the subway.　2　I don't like it when the subway gets really crowded.
3　One thing I don't like about this city is that there are always too many cars on the road.
4　I don't like spinach even though I know it's good for me.
5　I'm afraid you're a little too picky about food.　6　Why do you dislike him so much?
7　He doesn't like the idea of being controlled.　8　What's your favorite pastime?
9　I like to play tennis, but I'm not a very good player.
10　You have wonderful taste in movies.

45 취미와 관심사

STEP 1 통문장 말하기

661 제 취미는 액션 피규어 수집이에요. 당신은 취미가 있나요?
액션 피규어(만화 등에 나오는 캐릭터들을 축소해 만든 모형) action figure

662 사진 찍는 건 재미있는 취미라고 생각해요.
사진 촬영, 사진 찍기 photography

663 사진 찍기의 문제점은 돈이 많이 드는 취미라는 거예요.
비용이 많이 드는, 비싼 expensive

664 그건 아주 희귀한 피규어 세트네요. 그걸 모으는 데 얼마나 걸렸나요?
희귀한, 드문 rare

665 일 외에 특별한 관심사가 있나요?
~ 외에 other than   관심사 interest

STEP 2 통문장 외우기

My hobby is collecting action figures. Do you have a hobby?

I've thought photography would be an interesting hobby.

The trouble with photography is that it's an expensive hobby.

That's a rare set of figures. How long did it take you to collect them?

Do you have any special interests other than your job?

STEP 1 통문장 말하기

666 낚시에 흥미를 느끼게 됐어요.

667 정원 가꾸기가 긴장을 풀어주고 스트레스를 완화하는 것 같아요.
정원 가꾸기 gardening   긴장을 풀어주는 relaxing   완화하다 relieve

668 새로운 취미를 시작했어요. 늘 일만 하는 데 지쳤거든요.
지치다 get tired of

669 피아노 치는 법을 배우기 시작했어요.

670 저는 전문가가 아니에요. 재미 삼아 피아노를 쳐요.
전문가 professional   재미 삼아 for the fun of it

STEP 2 통문장 외우기

I've gotten interested in fishing.

I find gardening relaxing, and it relieves my stress.

I started a new hobby. I got tired of working all the time.

I started to learn how to play the piano.

I'm not a professional. I play the piano for the fun of it.

STEP 1   통문장 말하기

671 주말마다 좋은 책을 읽으면 일 생각을 안 하게 돼 좋아요.
~함으로써 by -ing   take A off B A를 B로부터 떨어뜨려 놓다

672 어떤 사람들은 취미로 스키 타는 걸 좋아하지만, 저는 골프 치는 게 더 좋아요.
~하는 것을 더 좋아하다 prefer -ing

673 외국어 공부는 제겐 그저 취미일 뿐이에요.

674 사촌은 연극 동아리 회원이에요. 그는 연기하는 것을 즐거워하는 것 같아요.
~인 것 같다 seem

675 희한한 취미들을 들어봤지만 그건 들어본 적이 없어요.
희한한, 특이한 unusual

STEP 2 통문장 외우기

On weekends, I like to take my mind off work by reading good books.

Some people like skiing, but I prefer golfing as a hobby.

Learning foreign languages is just a hobby for me.

My cousin is a member of a drama club. He seems to enjoy acting.

I've heard of unusual hobbies, but I've never heard of that one.

STEP 3 패턴으로 훈련하기

① My hobby is collecting [action figures / old books / antique* furniture]. Do you have a hobby?

*골동품의

② I've thought [photography / painting / cooking] would be an interesting hobby.

③ The trouble with [photography / traveling / sailing*] is that it's an expensive hobby.

*항해

④ That's a rare set of [figures / ancient plates* / antique chairs].

*접시

⑤ Do you have any special interests [other than / besides*] your job?

*~ 외에

⑥ I've gotten interested in fishing / drawing* / baking* .

*그리기, 데생
*빵 굽기

⑦ I find gardening / playing go* / calligraphy* relaxing, and it relieves my stress.

*바둑 두기
*캘리그래피, 서예

⑧ On weekends, I like to take my mind off work by reading good books / watching TV / going camping .

⑨ Some people like skiing, but I prefer golfing / surfing* / skydiving as a hobby.

*파도타기

⑩ Learning foreign languages / Taking classes in the humanities* / Building DIY* furniture is just a hobby for me.

*인문학
*직접 만들기(= Do It Yourself)

STEP 4 대화로 훈련하기

A Wow, that's a rare set of figures!
B ❶ 제 취미는 액션 피규어 수집이에요. 당신은 취미가 있나요?

A ❷ 사진 찍는 건 재미있는 취미라고 생각해요.
B The trouble with photography is that it's an expensive hobby.

A ❸ 일 외에 특별한 관심사가 있나요?
B I've gotten interested in fishing.

A It looks like you have been spending many hours in the garden.
B ❹ 정원 가꾸기가 긴장을 풀어주고 스트레스를 완화하는 것 같아요.

A ❺ 새로운 취미를 시작했어요. 늘 일만 하는 데 지쳤거든요.
B Tell me what it is.

A I heard you play the piano beautifully.
B ❻ 저는 전문가가 아니에요. 재미 삼아 피아노를 쳐요.

A ⑦ 주말마다 좋은 책을 읽으면 일 생각을 안 하게 돼 좋아요.

B I'm sorry, but reading books sounds boring to me.

A ⑧ 어떤 사람들은 취미로 스키 타는 걸 좋아하지만, 저는 골프 치는 게 더 좋아요.

B Golf is getting popular. It's not a luxury sport any more.

A Are you going to travel to China? Why are you studying Chinese?

B ⑨ 외국어 공부는 제겐 그저 취미일 뿐이에요.

A I heard some people collect parking tickets as a hobby.

B ⑩ 희한한 취미들을 들어봤지만 그건 들어본 적이 없어요.

ANSWERS!!

1 My hobby is collecting action figures. Do you have a hobby?
2 I've thought photography would be an interesting hobby.
3 Do you have any special interests other than your job?
4 I find gardening relaxing, and it relieves my stress.
5 I started a new hobby. I got tired of working all the time.
6 I'm not a professional. I play the piano for the fun of it.
7 On weekends, I like to take my mind off work by reading good books.
8 Some people like skiing, but I prefer golfing as a hobby.
9 Learning foreign languages is just a hobby for me.
10 I've heard of unusual hobbies, but I've never heard of that one.

46 스포츠 활동

STEP 1 통문장 말하기

676 놀 땐 주로 뭘 하세요?

677 야구는 제가 가장 좋아하는 스포츠예요. 당신은요?

678 제일 좋아하는 스포츠는 스키예요. 저는 스키 동아리 회원이에요.
~에 속하다 belong to

679 우리 가족은 지난 겨울에 처음으로 스키 타러 갔어요. 스키 장비를 사야 했어요.
장비 equipment

680 일주일에 세 번 개인 트레이너와 운동해요.
개인의 personal   운동하다 exercise

STEP 2 통문장 외우기

What do you like to do for fun?

Baseball is my favorite sport. What's yours?

My favorite sport is skiing. I belong to a ski club.

Our family went skiing last winter for the first time. We had to buy ski equipment.

I exercise 3 times a week with a personal trainer.

STEP 1　통문장 말하기

681　러닝머신 위보다 밖에서 달리는 게 더 좋아요.
러닝머신 treadmill

682　오늘 오후에 우리는 운동하러 체육관에 갔어요.
역기를 들었어요.
운동 workout
역기를 들다 lift weights

683　운동하는 바람에 근육이 쑤시네요.
운동하다 work out

684　조카는 야구 선수예요. 그는 투수예요.
투수 pitcher

685　야구를 했을 때 어떤 포지션에서 뛰었나요?

STEP 2 통문장 외우기

I like running outside better than on a treadmill.

This afternoon we went to the gym for a workout. We lifted weights.

My muscles are sore from working out.

My nephew is a baseball player. He is a pitcher.

When you played baseball, what position did you play?

STEP 1 통문장 말하기

686 우리는 어젯밤에 시합을 했어요. 점수는 6대 6 동점이었죠.
동점을 이루다, 비기다 tie

687 경기 규칙에 따라 시합해야 해요.
~에 따라 according to

688 가장 배우기 어려운 일은 깨끗이 승복하는 패자가 되는 거예요.

689 어젯밤 권투 경기에 갔어요. 좋은 시합이었죠.
권투, 복싱 boxing   시합 fight

690 오늘 축구 경기에 갈 생각 있어요?
축구 soccer

STEP 2 통문장 외우기

We played a game last night. The score was tied 6-6.

You should play according to the rules of the game.

The hardest thing to learn is to be a good loser.

I went to a boxing match last night. It was a good fight.

Would you be interested in going to a soccer match today?

STEP 3 패턴으로 훈련하기

❶ | Baseball / Basketball* / Tennis | is my favorite sport. What's yours?

*농구

❷ My favorite sport is | skiing / swimming / soccer |. I belong to a | ski / swimming / soccer | club.

❸ I exercise | 3 times a week / once a week / every two days* | with a personal trainer.

*이틀마다

❹ I like | running outside / jogging / working out at home | better than | on a treadmill / walking / at the gym |.

❺ My | muscles / legs / shoulders* | are sore from working out.

*어깨

⑥ My nephew is a baseball player. He   is a pitcher   .
                                        is a catcher*   *포수
                                        plays first base*   *1루

⑦ When you played   baseball   , what position did you play?
                    volleyball*   *배구
                    soccer

⑧ The score was   tied 6-6   .
                  7-6 in our favor*   *~에 유리하게
                  13-6 in their favor

⑨ I went to a   boxing match   last night.
                basketball game
                swimming meet*   *수영대회

⑩ Would you be interested in going to a   soccer match   today?
                                          horse race*   *경마
                                          hockey* match   *하키

STEP 4   대화로 훈련하기

A **① 놀 땐 주로 뭘 하세요?**
B I exercise with a personal trainer.

A What's your favorite sport?
B **② 제일 좋아하는 스포츠는 스키예요. 저는 스키 동아리 회원이에요.**

A Do you work out at a gym?
B **③ 러닝머신 위보다 밖에서 달리는 게 더 좋아요.**

A What's wrong with you?
B **④ 운동하는 바람에 근육이 쑤시네요.**

A **⑤ 조카는 야구 선수예요. 그는 투수예요.**
B Sounds cool. I'd like to see him play.

A **⑥ 야구를 했을 때 어떤 포지션에서 뛰었나요?**
B I played first base.

A When was your latest game?
B 우리는 어젯밤에 시합을 했어요. 점수는 6대 6 동점이었죠.

A 가장 배우기 어려운 일은 깨끗이 승복하는 패자가 되는 거예요.
B We didn't lose. They didn't play according to the rules.

A I called your house last night but you were away.
B 어젯밤 권투 경기에 갔어요. 좋은 시합이었죠.

A 오늘 축구 경기에 갈 생각 있어요?
B I'd really love to go.

ANSWERS!!

1. What do you like to do for fun?
2. My favorite sport is skiing. I belong to a ski club.
3. I like running outside better than on a treadmill.
4. My muscles are sore from working out.
5. My nephew is a baseball player. He is a pitcher.
6. When you played baseball, what position did you play?
7. We played a game last night. The score was tied 6-6.
8. The hardest thing to learn is to be a good loser.
9. I went to a boxing match last night. It was a good fight.
10. Would you be interested in going to a soccer match today?

DAY 47 음악 활동과 독서

STEP 1 통문장 말하기

691 가장 좋아하는 음악 장르는 뭔가요? 재즈 좋아하세요?

692 찰리 파커의 음악을 아주 좋아해요. 그는 제가 가장 좋아하는 뮤지션이에요.

693 그 곡을 전에 들어본 적이 없어요. 누가 작곡했나요?
  곡 piece

694 피아노를 훌륭하게 연주하시네요. 하루에 몇 시간 연습하세요?
  연습하다 practice

695 10년 가까이 피아노 레슨을 받았지만 이젠 연주하지 않아요.
  (의문문이나 부정문에서) 요즘은, 이제는 any more

STEP 2 통문장 외우기

What's your favorite kind of music?
Do you like jazz?

I like Charlie Parker's music a lot.
He's my favorite musician.

I've never heard that piece before.
Who wrote it?

You play the piano beautifully. How many hours a day do you practice?

I took piano lessons for nearly 10 years, but I don't play it any more.

STEP 1 통문장 말하기

696 우리는 교향악단의 연주를 들으러 음악회에 갔어요.
교향악단 symphony orchestra

697 극장 안의 모든 사람들이 기립 박수를 보냈어요.
기립 박수 standing ovation

698 추리 소설은 제가 가장 좋아하는 장르예요. 추리 소설은
추리 소설, 탐정 소설 detective fiction
모조리 읽어요.

699 이 소설의 저자는 누구죠?
저자, 작가 author

700 그 책에서 당신이 가장 좋아하는 부분이 뭔가요?

STEP 2 통문장 외우기

We went to a concert to hear the symphony orchestra.

Everyone in the theater gave it a standing ovation.

Detective fiction is my favorite genre. I read every detective novel I can.

Who is the author of this novel?

What is your favorite part of the book?

STEP 1 통문장 말하기

701 이 책이 너무 재미있어서 내려놓을 수가 없어요.
내려놓다 put down

702 흥미진진한 책이었어요. 밤새 읽었어요.
흥미진진한 책 page-turner   ~를 깨어 있게 하다 keep someone up

703 우리 시대의 가장 훌륭한 작가로 누구를 꼽겠어요?
이름을 대다 name

704 이 작가는 그의 저서에서 유머를 많이 구사하고 있어요.
저서, 저술물 writings

705 셰익스피어의 작품에 대해 얼마나 알고 있나요?
책, 작품 work

STEP 2 통문장 외우기

This book is so much fun that I can't put it down.

It was a page-turner. It kept me up all night.

Who would you name as the greatest author of our times?

This writer uses a lot of humor in his writings.

How much do you know about the works of Shakespeare?

STEP 3　패턴으로 훈련하기

❶ What's your favorite kind of music?

　Do you like　jazz　　　　　　?
　　　　　　　pop music*　　　　　　　　　　　　　　*대중 음악
　　　　　　　classical music*　　　　　　　　　　　*고전 음악
　　　　　　　hip-hop*　　　　　　　　　　　　　　*힙합 (음악)

❷ You play the　piano　beautifully.
　　　　　　　　violin
　　　　　　　　guitar

❸ I took　piano　lessons for nearly 10 years, but I don't play it
　　　　　flute
　　　　　drums　　　　　　　　　　　　　　　　any more.

❹ We went to a concert to hear　the symphony orchestra　.
　　　　　　　　　　　　　　　　a famous violinist
　　　　　　　　　　　　　　　　the world famous choir*　　*합창단

❺ Everyone in the theater　gave it a standing ovation　.
　　　　　　　　　　　　　clapped* at the end of the show
　　　　　　　　　　　　　called for* an encore performance*

손뼉을 치다/~을 요구하다/*앙코르 공연

❻ I read every [detective novel / fantasy novel / romance novel / non-fiction* book] I can.

*비소설, 실화

❼ Who is the author of this [novel / mystery story / essay]?

❽ This book is so [much fun / interesting / thrilling*] that I can't put it down.

*손에 땀을 쥐게 하는

❾ Who would you name as the greatest [author / writer / novelist*] of our times?

*소설가

❿ This writer uses [a lot of humor / vivid descriptions* / many metaphors*] in his writings.

*생생한 묘사
*은유, 비유

STEP 4 대화로 훈련하기

A ① 가장 좋아하는 음악 장르는 뭔가요?
B I'm into hip-hop these days.

A Do you like jazz?
B ② 찰리 파커의 음악을 아주 좋아해요. 그는 제가 가장 좋아하는 뮤지션이에요.

A How many hours a day do you practice?
B ③ 10년 가까이 피아노 레슨을 받았지만 이젠 연주하지 않아요.

A ④ 우리는 교향악단의 연주를 들으러 음악회에 갔어요.
B It's quite a surprise you like classical music.

A How was the concert?
B It was amazing. ⑤ 극장 안의 모든 사람들이 기립 박수를 보냈어요.

A What do you like to read?
B ⑥ 추리 소설은 제가 가장 좋아하는 장르예요. 추리 소설은 모조리 읽어요.

A **❼ 이 소설의 저자는 누구죠?**

B Are you serious? Even a child knows who wrote it.

A Hey, let's go out and have some fun.

B **❽ 이 책이 너무 재미있어서 내려놓을 수가 없어요.**

A **❾ 우리 시대의 가장 훌륭한 작가로 누구를 꼽겠어요?**

B I think no one can beat Joan Roawling.

A Why do people like the writer of this book?

B **❿ 이 작가는 그의 저서에서 유머를 많이 구사하고 있어요.**

ANSWERS!!

1 What's your favorite kind of music?
2 I like Charlie Parker's music a lot. He's my favorite musician.
3 I took piano lessons for nearly 10 years, but I don't play it any more.
4 We went to a concert to hear the symphony orchestra.
5 Everyone in the theater gave it a standing ovation.
6 Detective fiction is my favorite genre. I read every detective novel I can.
7 Who is the author of this novel?
8 This book is so much fun that I can't put it down.
9 Who would you name as the greatest author of our times?
10 This writer uses a lot of humor in his writings.

48 TV 시청

STEP 1 통문장 말하기

706 뭘 보는 중이에요?

707 저건 십 대들 사이에서 가장 인기 있는 프로그램이에요.
~ 중[사이]에서 among

708 우리는 인터넷으로 언제든지 이 프로그램을 다시 볼 수 있어요.

709 이 다큐멘터리는 무슨 내용인가요?
다큐멘터리 documentary

710 4차 산업 혁명에 관한 짧은 다큐멘터리예요.
산업 혁명 industrial revolution

STEP 2   통문장 외우기

What are you watching?

That is the most popular TV show among teenagers.

We can always watch this show again on the Internet.

What's this documentary about?

It's a short documentary about the 4th industrial revolution.

STEP 1 통문장 말하기

711 뉴스와 일기 예보 다음에 뭘 하나요?
일기 예보 weather forecast   방영하다 be on

712 그 요리 프로그램이 아직 방영되고 있는지 궁금하네요.
~인지 궁금하다 wonder if

713 요즘은 TV를 많이 보지 않아요.

714 보는 거라고는 지역 뉴스가 전부예요.

715 TV를 너무 많이 보면 게을러져요.
게으른 lazy

STEP 2 통문장 외우기

What's on after the news and the weather forecast?

I wonder if that cooking show is still on.

I don't watch a lot of TV anymore.

All I watch is the local news.

Watching too much TV makes you lazy.

STEP 1 통문장 말하기

716 소리 좀 키워주세요. 너무 작아요.
(볼륨을) 높이다, 올리다 turn up

717 채널 좀 그만 바꿔요. 한 채널에 고정해요.
~에 고정하다 stick to

718 TV 화면이 잘 안 나와요. 케이블 회사에 전화해야겠어요.
텔레비전 수상기 TV set

719 빌에게 당신 TV를 살펴보게 하세요. 아마 그가 고칠 수 있을 거예요.
살펴보다 look at   고치다, 수리하다 fix

720 다음에 새 TV를 살 때는 정말 좋은 걸로 살 거예요.

STEP 2 통문장 외우기

Please turn up the volume. It's too low.

Please stop changing the channel. Stick to one channel.

I can't get a good picture on my TV set. I need to call the cable company.

You ought to have Bill look at your TV. Maybe he can fix it.

The next time I buy a new TV, I'll buy a really good one.

STEP 3 패턴으로 훈련하기

❶ That is the most popular TV show among teenagers / women in their 20s / students in my class .

❷ What's this documentary / show / soap opera* about?   *드라마

❸ What's on after the news and the weather forecast / the sports feature* / the quiz show ?   *스포츠 특집 방송

❹ I wonder if that cooking show / cartoon* show / series is still on.   *만화

❺ All I watch is the local news / cartoons / daytime soaps* .   *주간 연속극

❻ Watching too much TV makes you lazy
kids violent*
people couch potatoes* .

폭력성 있는/ 장시간 TV만 보는 사람

❼ Please stop changing
switching* the channel. Stick to one channel.

*바꾸다

❽ I can't get a good
a clear*
any picture on my TV set.

*선명한

❾ You ought to have Bill look at your TV.

Maybe he can fix it
repair it
find out* what's wrong .

*알아내다

❿ The next time I buy a new TV, I'll buy a really good
the latest
a larger one.

STEP 4 대화로 훈련하기

A What are you watching?
B *Legion.* ❶ 저건 십 대들 사이에서 가장 인기 있는 프로그램이에요.

A Oh no! I've just missed my favorite TV show.
B ❷ 우리는 인터넷으로 언제든지 이 프로그램을 다시 볼 수 있어요.

A ❸ 이 다큐멘터리는 무슨 내용인가요?
B It's a short documentary about the 4th industrial revolution.

A ❹ 뉴스와 일기 예보 다음에 뭘 하나요?
B I have no idea. Check the channel guide.

A I like the cooking show on Olive TV.
B ❺ 그 요리 프로그램이 아직 방영되고 있는지 궁금하네요.

A ❻ 요즘은 TV를 많이 보지 않아요.
B Are you sure? I saw you watching a cartoon show.

A Do you like watching TV?
B ⑦ 보는 거라고는 지역 뉴스가 전부예요.

A Mom, why did you turn off the TV? I was watching.
B ⑧ TV를 너무 많이 보면 게을러져.

A ⑨ 채널 좀 그만 바꿔요. 한 채널에 고정해요.
B There's nothing fun on TV tonight.

A Honey, the TV screen is black again.
B ⑩ 다음에 새 TV를 살 때는 정말 좋은 걸로 살 거예요.

ANSWERS!!
1 That is the most popular TV show among teenagers.
2 We can always watch this show again on the Internet.
3 What's this documentary about?
4 What's on after the news and the weather forecast?
5 I wonder if that cooking show is still on.
6 I don't watch a lot of TV anymore.
7 All I watch is the local news.
8 Watching too much TV makes you lazy.
9 Please stop changing the channel. Stick to one channel.
10 The next time I buy a new TV, I'll buy a really good one.

49 뉴스와 미디어

STEP 1 통문장 말하기

721 오늘은 인터넷에 흥미로운 뉴스가 많지 않네요.

722 오늘 신문에 선거에 대한 기사가 났어요.
선거 election   기사 article

723 갇힌 광부들을 구조한 일에 관한 기사를 읽었나요?
갇힌 trapped 광부 miner   구조 rescue

724 그 기사를 전부 읽진 않았어요. 헤드라인만 슬쩍 봤어요.
전체의, 모든 whole   ~을 흘깃 보다 glance at

725 아침엔 보통 너무 바빠서 헤드라인만 대충 훑어봐요.
대충 훑어보다 scan

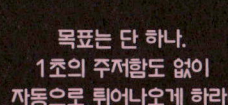

STEP 2　통문장 외우기

There isn't much interesting news on the Internet today.

There was an article in today's paper about the election.

Did you read the article about the rescue of the trapped miners?

I didn't read the whole article. I just glanced at the headlines.

I'm usually so busy in the morning that I just scan the headlines.

STEP 1 통문장 말하기

726 비즈니스 면을 찾고 있는 중이에요.
(신문의) 난(欄) section

727 매형이 《뉴욕 타임스》에 비즈니스 칼럼을 쓰고 있어요.
매형 brother-in-law   칼럼 column

728 사람들이 예전만큼 신문을 많이 읽는 것 같지 않아요.
~만큼 많이 as much as

729 휴대폰으로 뉴스를 읽을 수 있잖아요. 비용 면에서 효율적일 뿐만 아니라 편리하기도 하죠.
비용 효율이 높은 cost-effective
A뿐만 아니라 B도 B as well as A   편리한 convenient

730 여행 정보를 얻으려고 여행 잡지를 구매해요.

STEP 2 통문장 외우기

I'm looking for the business section.

My brother-in-law is writing a business column for the *New York Times*.

People don't seem to read the newspaper as much as before.

You can read news on your mobile. It's convenient as well as cost-effective.

I buy travel magazines to get travel information.

STEP 1 통문장 말하기

731 그 잡지를 구독하면 집이나 사무실로 배달될 거예요.
~을 구독하다 subscribe to

732 그 잡지의 구독 신청서를 보냈어요. 그 잡지는 매주 발간돼요.
구독 subscription ~을 발송하다 send in
발간되다, 나오다 come out

733 이 잡지를 얼마나 읽었어요?

734 그 잡지의 최신 호를 아직 못 봤어요. 벌써 나왔나요?
호 issue

735 프랑스의 유명 예술가의 이야기가 그 잡지 이번 호에 특집 기사로 실릴 거예요.
~을 특집 기사로 다루다 feature

STEP 2 통문장 외우기

If you subscribe to the magazine, it'll be delivered to your door or desk.

I sent in a subscription to the magazine. It comes out every week.

How long have you been reading this magazine?

I haven't seen the latest issue of the magazine. Is it out yet?

The story of a famous French artist will be featured in this issue of the magazine.

STEP 3 패턴으로 훈련하기

❶ There isn't much interesting news on the Internet / TV / the radio today.

❷ There was an article in today's paper about the election / earthquake* / bank robbery* .

*지진/*은행 강도

❸ Did you read the article about the rescue of the trapped miners / the earthquake in Tokyo / the 5-car chain collision* ?

*5중 충돌

❹ I didn't read the whole article. I just glanced at the headlines / first line / photos .

❺ I'm looking for the business / amusement* / editorial* section.

*연예
*사설

❻ It's convenient as well as cost-effective .
　　　　　　　　　　　　　　　 time-efficient*
　　　　　　　　　　　　　　　 simple to use

*시간 효율적인

❼ I buy travel   magazines to get travel information .
　　　　 business　　　　　　　 learn from business leaders
　　　　 fashion　　　　　　　　 learn about fashion trends*

*동향

❽ I sent in a subscription to the magazine.
　 It comes out   every week.
　　　 is issued
　　　 is released*

*발간되다

❾ How long have you been reading   this magazine?
　　　　　　　　　　　　　 subscribing to
　　　　　　　　　　　　　 taking

❿ The story of a famous French artist   will be featured in this
　　　　　　　　the Nobel Prize* winners
　　　　　　　　the Congo refugees*

*노벨상
*난민

issue of the magazine.

STEP 4 대화로 훈련하기

A Anything special this morning?
B ❶ 오늘은 인터넷에 흥미로운 뉴스가 많지 않네요.

A ❷ 오늘 신문에 선거에 대한 기사가 났어요.
B I'm not interested in politics at all.

A Did you read the article about the rescue of the trapped miners?
B ❸ 그 기사를 전부 읽진 않았어요. 헤드라인만 슬쩍 봤어요.

A ❹ 아침엔 보통 너무 바빠서 헤드라인만 대충 훑어봐요.
B That's why you always have incomplete information.

A What are you looking for?
B ❺ 비즈니스 면을 찾고 있는 중이에요. Our new products are featured on that section.

A ❻ 사람들이 예전만큼 신문을 많이 읽는 것 같지 않아요.
B Everybody reads news on their mobile phones.

A   What's the good point of reading news on your mobile?

B   ⑦ 비용 면에서 효율적일 뿐만 아니라 편리하기도 하죠.

A   Do you read any magazines?

B   ⑧ 여행 정보를 얻으려고 여행 잡지를 구매해요.

A   I need to buy a copy of *Time*, but I rarely have time to visit a book store.

B   ⑨ 그 잡지를 구독하면 집이나 사무실로 배달될 거예요.

A   ⑩ 그 잡지의 최신 호를 아직 못 봤어요. 벌써 나왔나요?

B   Check their Web site first.

ANSWERS!!

1. There isn't much interesting news on the Internet today.
2. There was an article in today's paper about the election.
3. I didn't read the whole article. I just glanced at the headlines.
4. I'm usually so busy in the morning that I just scan the headlines.
5. I'm looking for the business section.
6. People don't seem to read the newspaper as much as before.
7. It's convenient as well as cost-effective.
8. I buy travel magazines to get travel information.
9. If you subscribe to the magazine, it'll be delivered to your door or desk.
10. I haven't seen the latest issue of the magazine. Is it out yet?

DAY 50 글로벌 이슈

STEP 1 통문장 말하기

736 최근 인구 조사에 따르면 우리나라의 인구는 고령화되고 있어요.
인구 조사 census   나이를 먹다 age

737 65세 이상 인구가 빠르게 증가하고 있대요.
빠르게 늘어나다 grow fast

738 물가가 오르고 있어요. 1달러로는 아무것도 살 수 없어요.

739 내년에는 경제가 더 악화될 것 같아요.
경제 economy   더 나쁜 worse

740 실업률이 0.7퍼센트 증가했어요.
실업률 unemployment rate   ~만큼 오르다 rise by

STEP 2   통문장 외우기

According to the latest census, our population is aging.

They say the population aged 65 and older is growing fast.

Prices are going up. I can't buy anything for a dollar.

I'm afraid the economy will be worse next year.

The unemployment rate rose by 0.7 percent.

STEP 1 통문장 말하기

741 모두에게 돌아갈 정도로 일자리가 충분하진 않아요.
(사람들에게 몫이) 돌아가다 go around

742 중국의 빠른 경제 성장에 대해 어떻게 생각하세요?
빠른 rapid   경제 성장 economic growth

743 인구 증가가 그 성장에 큰 역할을 했다고 봐요.
~에 큰 역할을 하다 play a great role in

744 중국은 미국과의 무역에서 흑자를 내고 있어요.
무역 흑자를 내다 run a trade surplus

745 오늘 미국에서 새 대통령이 당선됐어요.
(선거로) 선출하다 elect

STEP 2 통문장 외우기

There aren't enough jobs to go around.

What do you think about China's rapid economic growth?

I see that the population growth played a great role in its growth.

China is running a trade surplus with America.

A new president was elected today in America.

STEP 1 통문장 말하기

746 미국의 새 대통령이 누군지 알아요?

747 미국에서 투표하려면 몇 살이 되어야 하나요?
투표하다 vote

748 전 세계에 나타난 최근의 폭염은 지구 온난화로 인한 것이에요.
전 세계에 around the globe   폭염 heat wave   지구 온난화 global warming

749 이러한 기후 변화는 지구와 생태계에 좋지 않아요.
생태계 ecosystem

750 700종 이상이 멸종 위기에 직면하고 있다고 들었어요.
종(種) species   멸종 extinction   직면하다 face

STEP 2 통문장 외우기

Do you know who the new president of the U.S. is?

How old do you have to be to vote in America?

Recent heat waves around the globe have been caused by global warming.

Such climate change is bad for the earth and its ecosystem.

I heard more than 700 species are facing extinction.

STEP 3 패턴으로 훈련하기

❶ According to the latest census, our population
- is aging
- has increased*
- has decreased*

*증가하다/*감소하다

❷ They say
- the population aged 65 and older
- the household debt*
- the divorce rate*

is growing fast.

*가계 부채
*이혼율

❸ Prices are
- going up
- getting too high
- skyrocketing*

. I can't buy anything for a dollar.

*급등하다

❹ I'm afraid the economy will
- be worse
- get weak*
- slow down*

next year.

*(통화·경제가) 약한
*(경제가) 위축되다

❺ The unemployment rate
- rose
- increased
- dropped

by 0.7 percent.

6 What do you think about | China's rapid economic growth | ?
gay marriage*
artificial intelligence*

*동성 결혼/*인공 지능

7 I see that | population growth | played a great role in its growth.
internet technology
the banking system

8 Do you know who the new | president | of | the U.S. | is?
mayor   New York
governor this state

9 How old do you have to be to | vote | in America?
drive a car
buy liquor*

*술

10 | Recent heat waves around the globe have | been caused
Natural disasters* have
The record rainfall* has

*재난, 재해
*기록적인 폭우

by global warming.

STEP 4 대화로 훈련하기

A ❶ 최근 인구 조사에 따르면 우리나라의 인구는 고령화되고 있어요.

B What's worse is that we have the world's fastest aging population.

A Why are many companies trying to make products for the elderly?

B ❷ 65세 이상 인구가 빠르게 증가하고 있대요.

A ❸ 물가가 오르고 있어요. 1달러로는 아무것도 살 수 없어요.

B After grocery shopping, I fear seeing the bill.

A ❹ 내년에는 경제가 더 악화될 것 같아요.

B I'm worried about that too.

A ❺ 실업률이 0.7 퍼센트 증가했어요.

B There aren't enough jobs to go around.

A What do you think about India's rapid economic growth?

B ❻ 인구 증가가 그 성장에 큰 역할을 했다고 봐요.

A ❼ 중국은 미국과의 무역에서 흑자를 내고 있어요.

B No wonder! It's hard to find anything not made in China.

A Why is "American president" on the search word ranking?

B ❽ 오늘 미국에서 새 대통령이 당선됐어요.

A ❾ 미국에서 투표하려면 몇 살이 되어야 하나요?

B I think it's 18.

A Recent heat waves around the globe have been caused by global warming.

B ❿ 이러한 기후 변화는 지구와 생태계에 좋지 않아요.

ANSWERS!!

1 According to the latest census, our population is aging.
2 They say the population aged 65 and older is growing fast.
3 Prices are going up. I can't buy anything for a dollar.
4 I'm afraid the economy will be worse next year.
5 The unemployment rate rose by 0.7 percent.
6 I see that the population growth played a great role in its growth.
7 China is running a trade surplus with America.
8 A new president was elected today in America.
9 How old do you have to be to vote in America?
10 Such climate change is bad for the earth and its ecosystem.

DAY 51 에피소드 말하기 1

STEP 1 통문장 말하기

751 오늘 아침 제게 이상한 일이 일어났어요.

752 길을 건너다가 하마터면 차에 치일 뻔했어요.

753 다행히 바로 뒤로 물러나서 차에 치이는 걸 피했어요.
뒤로 물러나다 back off   피하다 avoid

754 끔찍한 경험이어서 잊지 못할 거예요.
경험 experience

755 당신이 다치지 않아서 다행이에요.

STEP 2   통문장 외우기

A strange thing happened to me this morning.

I was crossing the street and was almost hit by a car.

Fortunately, I backed off in time to avoid being hit.

It was a terrible experience, and I won't forget it.

It's a good thing you didn't get hurt.

STEP 1 통문장 말하기

756 삼촌이 지난주에 심장 마비를 일으켰어요.
심장 마비, 심근경색 heart attack

757 그들은 심장 전문의를 불러야 했어요.
전문의 specialist

758 다음 날 의사가 그를 수술했어요.
~을 수술하다 operate on

759 수술은 잘됐어요. 걱정할 것 없어요.
잘되어가다 go well   걱정하다 worry

760 그가 빨리 회복하길 바랄 뿐이에요.
회복하다 get better

STEP 2 통문장 외우기

My uncle had a heart attack last week.

They had to call in a heart specialist.

The doctor operated on him the next day.

The operation went well. There's nothing to worry about.

I just hope he gets better soon.

STEP 1   통문장 말하기

761 미국 여행 이야기 좀 해주세요.

762 미국 얘기가 나와서 말인데, 뉴욕에서 어떤 일이
　　　~에 관해서 말하자면 speaking of
있었는지 제가 얘기한 적이 있나요?

763 길에서 옛 친구를 우연히 만났어요.
　　　　　　~를 우연히 만나다[마주치다] bump into

764 뉴욕에서 그녀를 만날 거라곤 전혀 상상하지
　　　　　　　　　　　　　　　　상상하다 imagine
못했어요.

765 우리는 당신이 의사가 될 거라곤 전혀 상상하지
못했어요.

STEP 2 통문장 외우기

Tell me about your trip to America.

Speaking of America, did I ever tell you about what happened in New York?

I bumped into an old friend on the street.

I never imagined that I would be seeing her in New York.

We never imagined that you would become a doctor.

STEP 3 패턴으로 훈련하기

❶ | A strange | thing happened to me this morning.
   | An odd* |
   | A funny |

*이상한

❷ I was crossing the street and was almost hit by a | car | .
                                                    | truck |
                                                    | motorcycle* |

*오토바이

❸ Fortunately, I | backed off | in time to avoid being hit.
                 | got out of the way |
                 | realized the danger* |

*위험

❹ It was a terrible | experience | , and I won't forget it.
                    | situation* |
                    | memory* |

*상황
*기억

❺ My uncle had | a heart attack | last week.
               | the flu* |
               | food poisoning* |

*독감
*식중독

⑥ The doctor [operated on him / injected* him with an antibiotic* / prescribed* medicine for him] the next day.
*주사하다/*항생제
*처방하다

⑦ There's nothing to [worry about / be concerned about* / be afraid of].
*~에 대해 걱정하다

⑧ [Speaking of / Talking about / As for*] America, did I ever tell you about what happened in New York?
*~에 대해 말하자면

⑨ I never imagined that I would be [seeing her in New York / married to her / living in Kenya].

⑩ We never [imagined / thought / expected] that you would become a doctor.

STEP 4 대화로 훈련하기

A ❶ 오늘 아침 제게 이상한 일이 일어났어요.
B What happened? Give it to me.

A ❷ 길을 건너다가 하마터면 차에 치일 뻔했어요.
B It's a good thing you didn't get hurt.

A I'm sorry to hear that there was a fire in your house.
B ❸ 끔찍한 경험이어서 잊지 못할 거예요.

A I was wondering why you left the office so early last week.
B ❹ 삼촌이 지난주에 심장 마비를 일으켰어요.

A How was the operation?
B ❺ 수술은 잘됐어요. 걱정할 것 없어요.

A My son has food poisoning, so he can't go to school.
B ❻ 그가 빨리 회복하길 바랄 뿐이에요.

A ❼ 미국 여행 이야기 좀 해주세요.

B I really enjoyed it. It was the happiest time of my life.

A ❽ 미국 얘기가 나와서 말인데, 뉴욕에서 어떤 일이 있었는지 제가 얘기한 적이 있나요?

B I'm sorry, but I've heard enough about your life in New York.

A Why are you in such a good mood today?

B ❾ 길에서 옛 친구를 우연히 만났어요.

A ❿ 뉴욕에서 그녀를 만날 거라곤 전혀 상상하지 못했어요.

B It's a small world, isn't it?

ANSWERS!!

1. A strange thing happened to me this morning.
2. I was crossing the street and was almost hit by a car.
3. It was a terrible experience, and I won't forget it.
4. My uncle had a heart attack last week.
5. The operation went well. There's nothing to worry about.
6. I just hope he gets better soon.
7. Tell me about your trip to America.
8. Speaking of America, did I ever tell you about what happened in New York?
9. I bumped into an old friend on the street.
10. I never imagined that I would be seeing her in New York.

DAY 52 에피소드 말하기 2

STEP 1 통문장 말하기

766 오늘 아침 건강 검진을 받으러 갔어요.
건강 검진 medical check-up

767 그들은 저의 흉부 엑스레이를 찍고 혈압을 쟀어요.
흉부, 가슴 chest   혈압 blood pressure

768 의사는 제가 좀 과체중이라고 했어요.
과체중의, 비만의 overweight

769 그는 저에게 고혈압이 있다고도 했어요.
고혈압 high blood pressure

770 그는 제게 암에 대한 가족력이 있냐고 물었어요.
암 cancer   (개인·가정의) 이력, 내력 history

STEP 2 통문장 외우기

I went for a medical check-up this morning.

They gave me a chest X-ray and took my blood pressure.

The doctor said I'm a little overweight.

He also said I have high blood pressure.

He asked me if there is a history of cancer in my family.

STEP 1　통문장 말하기

771 그는 제게 운동을 많이 하라고 조언했어요.
많은 plenty of　　조언하다 advise

772 흡연 역시 당신 건강에 해로운 것 같아요.
(건강에) 해로운[유해한] harmful

773 어제는 날이 좋아서 우리는 드라이브를 가기로 했어요.

774 피크닉 점심을 준비해서 강가에서 드라이브했어요.
준비하다 prepare

775 잠시 후 우리는 나무 아래 그늘진 곳을 발견했어요.
잠시 후 after a while　　그늘이 드리워진 shady

STEP 2 통문장 외우기

He advised me to get plenty of exercise.

I think smoking is also harmful to your health.

Yesterday was a beautiful day, we decided to go for a drive.

We prepared a picnic lunch and drove down by the river.

After a while, we found a shady place under some trees.

STEP 1 통문장 말하기

776 거기에 있는 동안 우리는 아주 즐거웠어요.
~하는 동안 while

777 하지만 안 좋은 일이 일어날 것 같았어요.

778 집에 돌아오는 길에 타이어에 펑크가 났어요.
돌아가는 길에 on the way back   타이어에 펑크가 나다 have a flat tire

779 돌아왔을 땐 어두워진 뒤였고 우린 모두 지쳤어요.
어두워진 후 after dark

780 힘든 하루를 보낸 것 같네요.
힘든 rough

STEP 2 통문장 외우기

We had a lot of fun while we were there.

But I felt something bad was going to happen.

On the way back home, we had a flat tire.

It was after dark when we got back, and we were all tired.

It sounds like you had a rough day.

STEP 3 패턴으로 훈련하기

❶ I went for a medical check-up this morning.
　　　　　　 a physical examination*
　　　　　　 an eye examination

*신체검사
*시력 검사

❷ They gave me a chest X-ray and took my blood pressure .
　　　　　　　　　　　　　　　　　　 my temperature*
　　　　　　　　　　　　　　　　　　 a blood sample*

*체온
*혈액 샘플

❸ The doctor said I'm a little overweight .
　　　　　　　　　　　　　　　underweight*
　　　　　　　　　　　　　　　near-sighted*
　　　　　　　　　　　　　　　far-sighted*

*표준 체중 이하의
*근시(近視)의
*원시(遠視)의

❹ He asked me if there is a history of cancer in my family .
　　　　　　　　 I am currently* taking any medication
　　　　　　　　 I have had any operations in the past

*현재에

❺ He advised me to get plenty of exercise .
　　　　　　　　　 lose weight*
　　　　　　　　　 change my diet*

*살을 빼다
*식습관, 식단

132

6. Yesterday was a [beautiful / bright / perfect] day, we decided to go for a drive.

7. After a while, we found a shady place [under / near / by] some trees.

8. We had a [lot of fun / good time / boring* time] while we were there.

*지루한

9. On the way back home, we had [a flat tire / some engine trouble / a breakdown*].

*고장

10. It was after dark when we got back, and we were all [tired / exhausted* / worn-out*].

진이 빠진/ 매우 지친

STEP 4　대화로 훈련하기

A　❶ 오늘 아침 건강 검진을 받으러 갔어요.

B　Any problems? You look as healthy as a horse.

A　Did they give you a full workup*?　　　*종합 검진

B　No, ❷ 그들은 저의 흉부 엑스레이를 찍고 혈압을 쟀어요.

A　❸ 의사는 제가 좀 과체중이라고 했어요.

B　Eat more slowly. It helps you feel full.

A　What else did the doctor ask you?

B　❹ 그는 제게 암에 대한 가족력이 있냐고 물었어요.

A　❺ 그는 제게 운동을 많이 하라고 조언했어요.

B　You need to move your body even at work.

A　I've decided to quit drinking.

B　❻ 흡연 역시 당신 건강에 해로운 것 같아요.

A ⑦ 어제는 날이 좋아서 우리는 드라이브를 가기로 했어요.

B It was a good day to drive around.

A How was your first date?

B Fantastic! ⑧ 피크닉 점심을 준비해서 강가에서 드라이브했어요.

A Why did it take so long to get here?

B ⑨ 집에 돌아오는 길에 타이어에 펑크가 났어요.

A ⑩ 힘든 하루를 보낸 것 같네요.

B I'm really exhausted.

ANSWERS!!

1 I went for a medical check-up this morning.
2 they gave me a chest X-ray and took my blood pressure.
3 The doctor said I'm a little overweight.
4 He asked me if there is a history of cancer in my family.
5 He advised me to get plenty of exercise.
6 I think smoking is also harmful to your health.
7 Yesterday was a beautiful day, we decided to go for a drive.
8 We prepared a picnic lunch and drove down by the river.
9 On the way back home, we had a flat tire.
10 It sounds like you had a rough day.

DAY 53 앞으로의 일 가정하기

STEP 1 통문장 말하기

781 내일 비가 안 오면 쇼핑하러 가려고요.

782 우리가 갈지 모르지만 전적으로 날씨에 달려 있어요.
　　　　　가능한 일, 가능성 possibility

783 내일 시간이 되면 머리를 자르려고요.
　　　　　머리를 깎다 get a haircut

784 미용사에게 머리를 너무 짧게 자르지 말라고 요청하는 걸 기억해야 해요.

785 아들은 자라서 경찰관이 되고 싶어 해요.

STEP 2 통문장 외우기

If it doesn't rain tomorrow, I think I'll go shopping.

There's a possibility we'll go, but it all depends on the weather.

If I have time tomorrow, I think I'll get a haircut.

You should remember to ask the hair stylist not to cut your hair too short.

My son wants to be a police officer when he grows up.

STEP 1 통문장 말하기

786 그에게 정말 경찰관이 되고 싶다면 더 열심히 공부해야 한다고 말해주세요.
더 열심히 harder

787 가까운 시일 내에 휴가를 가고 싶어요.
가까운 시일 내에, 조만간 one of these days

788 일을 제때 마치면 월요일에 뉴욕으로 떠날 거예요.

789 그 여행을 못 가게 됐다고 가정해보세요. 어떻게 하시겠어요?
~라고 가정하다 suppose

790 당신과 함께 간다면 6시까지 돌아와야 할 거예요.
돌아오다 be back

STEP 2 통문장 외우기

Tell him he should study harder if he really wants to be a police officer.

One of these days, I'd like to take a vacation.

If I get my work finished in time, I'll leave for New York on Monday.

Suppose you can't go on the trip. What would you do?

If I go with you, I'll have to be back by 6 o'clock.

STEP 1 통문장 말하기

791 당신과 같이 갈 수 없다고 말한다면 뭐라고 할 거예요?

792 저 차를 사려면 돈을 좀 빌려야 할 거예요.
빌리다 borrow

793 어떤 식으로든 우리가 당신을 도울 수 있을지도 몰라요.
어떻게 해서든, 어떻게든 in some way

794 가능한 한 빨리 직업을 바꿀 거예요.
가능한 한 빨리 as soon as someone can

795 그가 크리스마스에 집에 못 올지도 몰라요.
~일지도 모른다 there's a chance

STEP 2 통문장 외우기

What would you say if I told you I couldn't go with you?

If I buy that car, I'll have to borrow some money.

We may be able to help you in some way.

As soon as I can, I'm going to change jobs.

There's a chance he won't be able to come home for Christmas.

STEP 3 패턴으로 훈련하기

❶ If it doesn't rain tomorrow, I think I'll go
- shopping
- hiking
- on a picnic

❷ There's a possibility we'll go, but it all depends on
- the weather
- the work schedule
- your bank balance*

*은행 잔고

❸ If I have time tomorrow, I think I'll
- get a haircut
- get my hair dyed*
- go to the beauty salon

*염색된

❹ You should remember to ask the hair stylist not to
- cut your hair too short
- give your hair too many curls
- make your hair color too bright

❺ My son wants to be
- a police officer
- a scientist
- an astronaut*

when he grows up.

*우주 비행사

❻ One of these days, I'd like to take a vacation .
　　　　　　　　　　　　　　　　 buy a new car
　　　　　　　　　　　　　　　　 throw a party*

*파티를 열다

❼ Suppose   you can't go on the trip. What would you do?
　 Let's suppose
　 Let's say*
　 Assume*

*예를 들면

*~라고 가정하다

❽ What would you say if I told you I couldn't go with you?
　 What would you do
　 How would you feel

❾ We may be able to help you   in some way.
　　　　　　　　　　 support you
　　　　　　　　　　 give you a hand*

*도와주다

❿ There's a chance he won't be able to
　　　　　　　　　　　　　　　　　　 come home for Christmas .
　　　　　　　　　　　　　　　　　　 get any day off* for the holidays
　　　　　　　　　　　　　　　　　　 make it for the meeting today

*휴가를 내다

STEP 4 대화로 훈련하기

A   Do you have any plans for tomorrow?

B   ❶ 내일 비가 안 오면 쇼핑하러 가려고요.

A   Your hair looks messy. Why don't you take some time to visit the beauty salon?

B   ❷ 내일 시간이 되면 머리를 자르려고요.

A   ❸ 미용사에게 머리를 너무 짧게 자르지 말라고 요청하는 걸 기억해야 해요.

B   Don't you know short hair really suits me?

A   My son wants to be a police officer when he grows up.

B   ❹ 그에게 정말 경찰관이 되고 싶다면 더 열심히 공부해야 한다고 말해주세요.

A   ❺ 일을 제때 마치면 월요일에 뉴욕으로 떠날 거예요.

B   I'll cross my fingers* for you!

*행운을 빌다

A   ❻ 그 여행을 못 가게 됐다고 가정해보세요. 어떻게 하시겠어요?

B   I would reschedule my travel plans.

A Would you like to go out tonight?
B ⑦ 당신과 같이 갈 수 없다고 말한다면 뭐라고 할 거예요?

A Look at that hybrid model! Isn't it time to replace your car?
B ⑧ 저 차를 사려면 돈을 좀 빌려야 할 거예요.

A ⑨ 가능한 한 빨리 직업을 바꿀 거예요.
B We may be able to help you in some way.

A I'm so excited to see my little nephew this Christmas.
B ⑩ 그가 크리스마스에 집에 못 올지도 몰라요.

ANSWERS!!

1 If it doesn't rain tomorrow, I think I'll go shopping.
2 If I have time tomorrow, I think I'll get a haircut.
3 You should remember to ask the hair stylist not to cut your hair too short.
4 Tell him he should study harder if he really wants to be a police officer.
5 If I get my work finished in time, I'll leave for New York on Monday.
6 Suppose you can't go on the trip. What would you do?
7 What would you say if I told you I couldn't go with you?
8 If I buy that car, I'll have to borrow some money.
9 As soon as I can, I'm going to change jobs.
10 There's a chance he won't be able to come home for Christmas.

DAY 54 과거에 대한 아쉬움과 후회

STEP 1 통문장 말하기

796 비가 오지 않았다면 소풍을 갔을 거예요.
~했을 것이다 would have p.p.

797 공부할 필요가 없었다면 어젯밤에 뭘 했을 거예요?

798 더 일찍 일어났다면 아침 식사할 시간이 있었을 거예요.

799 시간이 있었으면 당신에게 전화했을 거예요.

800 제가 부탁했던 대로 당신이 제게 전화를 걸었으면 좋았을 텐데요.
~면 좋겠다 I wish

STEP 2 통문장 외우기

I would have gone on the picnic, if it hadn't rained.

What would you have done last night if you hadn't needed to study?

If you had gotten up earlier, you would have had time for breakfast.

If I had had time, I would have called you.

I wish you had called me back, as I had asked you to.

STEP 1 통문장 말하기

801 제 입장이었다면 똑같이 했겠어요?
~의 입장이 되어 in one's shoes

802 그가 광고를 더 빨리 보기만 했어도 그 집을 샀을 거예요.
광고 advertisement

803 당신이 더 조심했다면 다리가 부러지진 않았겠죠.

804 그가 가고 싶어 한 걸 알았으면 전화했을 거예요.

805 그는 당신과 가려고 했는데 시간이 없었어요.

STEP 2 통문장 외우기

Would you have done the same if you had been in my shoes?

If he had only seen the advertisement sooner, he would have bought that house.

If you had been more careful, you wouldn't have broken your leg.

If I had known he wanted to go, I would have called him.

He would have gone with you, but he didn't have time.

STEP 1   통문장 말하기

806   문을 잠그지 말아야 했어요.
~해야 했다 should have p.p.

807   당신은 길을 물어봐야 했어요, 그럼 길을 잃지
길을 물어보다 ask for directions   길을 잃다 get lost
않았겠죠.

808   당신의 도움이 없었더라면 큰 어려움에 처했을지도
~했을지도 모른다 might have p.p.
몰라요.

809   당신이 그 말을 하지 않았더라면 모든 게 괜찮았을
괜찮은, 무사한 all right
거예요.

810   그 일을 돌아보니 당신에게 모든 걸 말하지 않았으면
~을 되돌아보다 look back on
좋았을 거예요.

STEP 2 통문장 외우기

I shouldn't have locked the door.

You should have asked for directions, and you wouldn't have gotten lost.

Without your help, I might have been in big trouble.

Everything would have been all right if you hadn't said that.

Looking back on it, I wish I hadn't told you everything.

STEP 3　패턴으로 훈련하기

❶ I would have gone on the picnic, if
   > it hadn't rained
   > you had told me about it earlier
   > I had known you were going

❷ What would you have done last night if you hadn't needed to
   > study
   > work
   > go to the gym
   ?

❸ If you had
   > gotten up earlier
   > hurried up
   > gotten dressed quickly
   , you would have had time for breakfast.

❹ If I had had time, I would have
   > called you
   > helped you with the paperwork*
   > seen all my old friends
   .

   *문서 업무

❺ I wish you had
   > called me back
   > visited me
   > finished your work
   , as I had asked you to.

152

❻ If I had known he wanted to go, I would have called him .
 invited him
 counted him in*

*~을 끼워주다

❼ I shouldn't have locked the door .
 bothered* you
 married her

*귀찮게 하다

❽ Without your help, I might have been in big trouble .
 lost my way*
 failed the project

*길을 잃다

❾ Everything would have been all right if you hadn't said that.
 settled*
 perfect

*(논쟁 등을) 끝내다, 합의를 보다

❿ Looking back on it , I wish I hadn't told you everything.
 Now that I think about it
 Come to think of it*

*그러고 보니

STEP 4　대화로 훈련하기

A　Why are you home all day?
B　❶ 비가 오지 않았다면 소풍을 갔을 거예요.

A　Is it time for lunch yet? I'm starving to death*.　　*배고파 죽겠어요.
B　❷ 더 일찍 일어났다면 아침 식사할 시간이 있었을 거예요.

A　❸ 제가 부탁했던 대로 당신이 전화를 걸었으면 좋았을 텐데요.
B　I forgot but I promise I'll never do it again.

A　I'm sorry but can we put this behind us*?　*put something behind someone ~을 없던 일로 하다
B　❹ 제 입장이었다면 똑같이 했겠어요?

A　I slipped on ice and broke my leg.
B　❺ 당신이 더 조심했다면 다리가 부러지진 않았겠죠.

A　❻ 그가 가고 싶어 한 걸 알았으면 전화했을 거예요.
B　It's your fault. You should have asked him first.

A Did you leave the keys in your car again?
B ❼ 문을 잠그지 말아야 했어요.

A I was lost in downtown Paris for 3 hours.
B ❽ 당신은 길을 물어봐야 했어요, 그럼 길을 잃지 않았겠죠.

A ❾ 당신의 도움이 없었더라면 큰 어려움에 처했을지도 몰라요.
B I'm happy to help.

A ❿ 그 일을 돌아보니 당신에게 모든 걸 말하지 않았으면 좋았을 거예요.
B Please forgive me. That was so stupid of me.

ANSWERS!!

1 I would have gone on the picnic, if it hadn't rained.
2 If you had gotten up earlier, you would have had time for breakfast.
3 I wish you had called me back, as I had asked you to.
4 Would you have done the same if you had been in my shoes?
5 If you had been more careful, you wouldn't have broken your leg.
6 If I had known he wanted to go, I would have called him.
7 I shouldn't have locked the door.
8 You should have asked for directions, and you wouldn't have gotten lost.
9 Without your help, I might have been in big trouble.
10 Looking back on it, I wish I hadn't told you everything.

DAY 55 정중한 부탁과 요청

STEP 1 통문장 말하기

811 문이 닫히지 않게 잡아주시겠어요?
~이 닫히지 않게 잡다 hold ~ open

812 불을 꺼주시면 고맙겠습니다.
끄다 turn out   고마워하다 appreciate

813 저를 돕는 데 수고해주시니 정말 친절하시네요.
수고를 아끼지 않다 take the trouble

814 제 차를 밀어주시지 않겠어요? 차가 멈췄어요.
~을 밀다 give ~ a push   멈추다, 정지하다 stall

815 당신의 친절에 어떻게든 보답할 수 있으면 좋겠네요.
어떻게든 somehow   보답하다 repay

STEP 2 통문장 외우기

Would you please hold the door open for me?

I'd appreciate it if you would turn out the lights.

You're very kind to take the trouble to help me.

Would you mind giving my car a push? It has stalled.

I wish I could repay you somehow for your kindness.

STEP 1 통문장 말하기

816 너무 성가신 일은 아니었길 바라요.
성가신 일 bother

817 조금도 귀찮지 않았어요. 기쁜 마음으로 그 일을 했는걸요.

818 마지막으로 부탁드릴 일이 딱 하나 있어요.
부탁하다 ask a favor

819 할 수 있다면 어떤 식으로든 기꺼이 도와드리겠어요.

820 이 창문을 열어주시겠어요? 문이 꼼짝 안 하네요.
꼼짝 못하는, 움직일 수 없는 stuck

STEP 2 통문장 외우기

I hope it wasn't too much of a bother.

It wasn't any bother. I was glad to do it.

There's just one last favor I need to ask of you.

I'd be happy to help you in any way I can.

Would you open this window for me? It's stuck.

STEP 1 통문장 말하기

821 제가 할 수 있는 게 또 있다면 알려주세요.
~에게 알리다[말하다] let ~ know

822 이번이 뭘 해달라고 하는 마지막 부탁이에요.

823 10달러만 빌려주시겠어요? 집에 지갑을 두고 왔네요.
빌려주다 lend

824 그는 당신이 한 일에 대해 늘 감사할 거예요.
(도움을 준) ~에게 매우 감사하다 be indebted to

825 그렇게 많은 불편을 드릴 의도는 분명 없었어요.
불편 inconvenience   분명히, 틀림없이 certainly

STEP 2　통문장 외우기

If there's anything else I can do, please let me know.

This is the last time I'll ever ask you to do anything for me.

Could you lend me 10 dollars? I left my wallet at home.

He'll always be indebted to you for what you've done.

I certainly didn't intend to cause you so much inconvenience.

STEP 3 패턴으로 훈련하기

❶ Would you please **hold the door open / leave this window closed / have dinner ready** for me?

❷ I'd appreciate it if you would **turn out the lights / try to be quiet / not talk so loudly**.

❸ You're very **kind / sweet / thoughtful*** to take the trouble to help me.

*배려 있는

❹ Would you mind **giving my car a push / opening the door / lending me some money**?

❺ I wish I could **repay / reward* / thank*** you somehow for your kindness.

*보답하다
*감사를 표하다

⑥ It wasn't [any bother / any trouble / anything at all]. I was glad to do it.

⑦ There's just one last favor [I need / I'd like / I just have] to ask of you.

⑧ I'd be happy to help you in any way I [can / am able to / might be able to].

⑨ If there's anything else I can do, please [let me know / tell me / don't hesitate* to ask me].

*주저하다

⑩ This is the last time I'll ever ask you [to do anything for me / to do me a favor / for favors].

STEP 4 대화로 훈련하기

A ① 문이 닫히지 않게 잡아주시겠어요?

B Sure. Do you want me to help you with the bags?

A Are you going to bed now?

B ② 불을 꺼주시면 고맙겠습니다.

A ③ 저를 돕는 데 수고해주시니 정말 친절하시네요.

B It was nothing.

A ④ 제 차를 밀어주시지 않겠어요? 차가 멈췄어요.

B Of course not. I'll help you out.

A I hope it wasn't too much of a bother.

B ⑤ 조금도 귀찮지 않았어요. 기쁜 마음으로 그 일을 했는걸요.

A ⑥ 마지막으로 부탁드릴 일이 딱 하나 있어요.

B Are you sure it's really the last?

A **할 수 있다면 어떤 식으로든 기꺼이 도와드리겠어요.**

B You're my hero.

A Thanks for lending a hand*. You've been so helpful. *도와주다

B **제가 할 수 있는 게 또 있다면 알려주세요.**

A **10달러만 빌려주시겠어요? 집에 지갑을 두고 왔네요.**

B You've done it again?

A **그렇게 많은 불편을 드릴 의도는 분명 없었어요.**

B No worries. The pleasure was mine.

ANSWERS!!

1. Would you please hold the door open for me?
2. I'd appreciate it if you would turn out the lights.
3. You're very kind to take the trouble to help me.
4. Would you mind giving my car a push? It has stalled.
5. It wasn't any bother. I was glad to do it.
6. There's just one last favor I need to ask of you.
7. I'd be happy to help you in any way I can.
8. If there's anything else I can do, please let me know.
9. Could you lend me 10 dollars? I left my wallet at home.
10. I certainly didn't intend to cause you so much inconvenience.

DAY 56 회의와 발표

STEP 1 통문장 말하기

826 우리가 회의 일정을 변경할 수 있을지 궁금해하고 있었어요.
일정을 변경하다 reschedule

827 회의가 금요일로 미뤄졌어요.
미루다, 연기하다 postpone

828 금요일에 발표하기로 되어 있어요.
~하기로 되어 있다 be supposed to

829 이사들에게 회의 안건을 나눠주시겠어요?
이사진 board members   안건 agenda   나눠주다 hand out

830 우린 모두들 그 메모를 받았는지 확인할 필요가 있어요.
받다 receive

STEP 2　통문장 외우기

I was wondering if we could reschedule the meeting.

The meeting has been postponed to Friday.

I'm supposed to make a presentation on Friday.

Could you please hand out the agenda to the board members?

We need to make sure everyone has received the memo.

STEP 1 통문장 말하기

831 모두 저와 함께 첸 씨를 환영해주시겠어요?
환영하다, 맞이하다 welcome

832 우리는 새로운 마케팅 전략을 논의하고자 오늘 이 자리에 왔습니다.
전략 strategy

833 텔레마케팅은 성공을 보장하지 못해요.
보장하다 guarantee

834 소셜 네트워크 서비스가 점점 더 흔해지고 있어요.
흔한 commonplace

835 이 상품은 인터넷으로 마케팅해볼 가치가 있다고 봐요.
~할 가치가 있는 worth

STEP 2 통문장 외우기

Would you please join me in welcoming Ms. Chen?

We are here today to discuss new marketing strategies.

Telemarketing cannot guarantee success.

Social Networking Services have become more commonplace.

I think it's worth trying Web marketing with this product.

STEP 1   통문장 말하기

836   그것에 대해 좀 더 자세히 말씀해주시겠어요?
자세히 설명하다 go into detail(s)

837   발표할 기회를 주셔서 정말 감사합니다.
발표하다 present

838   그녀의 발표는 꽤 인상적이었어요. 핵심이 정확했고 효율적이었죠.
핵심을 찌르는 to the point
효율적인 efficient

839   그녀가 우리 팀의 귀중한 자산이 될 것이라고 확신해요.
자산, 재산 asset

840   팀 전체가 공을 인정받아야 할 것 같아요.
공적을 인정받다 take credit

STEP 2 통문장 외우기

Can you go into more detail about that?

Thank you so much for the chance to present.

Her presentation was quite impressive. It was to the point and efficient.

I'm sure she will be a great asset to our team.

I think the whole team should take credit.

STEP 3 패턴으로 훈련하기

❶ I was wondering if we could | reschedule / cancel / postpone | the meeting.

❷ I'm supposed to | make a presentation / attend the meeting / meet a client* over lunch | on Friday.

*고객

❸ Could you please hand out the | agenda / document / minutes* | to the board members?

*회의록

❹ We need to make sure | everyone has received the memo / the project is on schedule / the conference room has been reserved* |.

*예약하다

❺ We are here today to discuss | new marketing strategies / last year's sales figures* / launching* a new product |.

*매출액
*출시하다

❻ **Telemarketing** cannot guarantee success.
This approach
Traditional* management system

*전통적인

❼ I think it's worth **trying Web marketing with this product**.
surveying* the market
negotiating* the price

*조사하다/*협상하다

❽ Thank you so much for **the chance to present**.
attending
listening

❾ Her presentation was **quite impressive**.
clearly organized*
very informative*

*정리된
*유익한

❿ I'm sure she **will be a great asset** to our team.
is a real asset
is indispensable*

*없어서는 안 되는

STEP 4 대화로 훈련하기

A 　**우리가 회의 일정을 변경할 수 있을지 궁금해하고 있었어요.**
B 　When would you like to reschedule it for?

A 　We have a meeting this afternoon, don't we?
B 　**회의가 금요일로 미뤄졌어요.**

A 　**금요일에 발표하기로 되어 있어요.** I'm so nervous.
B 　I know how you feel, but you can do it.

A 　I sent a memo to the board members yesterday.
B 　**우린 모두들 그 메모를 받았는지 확인할 필요가 있어요.**

A 　**텔레마케팅은 성공을 보장하지 못해요.**
B 　I couldn't agree with you more.*   *전적으로 찬성해요.

A 　**이 상품은 인터넷으로 마케팅해볼 가치가 있다고 봐요.**
B 　Excellent! We should look into* that.   *조사하다

A ⑦ 그것에 대해 좀 더 자세히 말씀해주시겠어요?

B I'll get to that in a minute.

A ⑧ 발표할 기회를 주셔서 정말 감사합니다.

B You did a good job.

A ⑨ 그녀의 발표는 꽤 인상적이었어요. 핵심이 정확했고 효율적이었죠.

B You're right. She's doing great.

A Your presentation was outstanding. I'm sure you will be a great asset to our team.

B ⑩ 팀 전체가 공을 인정받아야 할 것 같아요.

ANSWERS!!

1 I was wondering if we could reschedule the meeting.
2 The meeting has been postponed to Friday.
3 I'm supposed to make a presentation on Friday.
4 We need to make sure everyone has received the memo.
5 Telemarketing cannot guarantee success.
6 I think it's worth trying Web marketing with this product.
7 Can you go into more detail about that?
8 Thank you so much for the chance to present.
9 Her presentation was quite impressive. It was to the point and efficient.
10 I think the whole team should take credit.

DAY 57 의견 묻고 답하기

STEP 1 통문장 말하기

841 어떻게 생각해요? 그게 맞나요?

842 물론이죠. 그 점에 대해선 당신이 전적으로 옳아요.
전적으로, 틀림없이 absolutely

843 그 점에 있어선 당신이 잘못 알고 있는 것 같네요.
잘못 알고 있는 mistaken

844 신입 사원에 대해 어떻게 생각해요?
직원 employee

845 그는 성격이 매우 좋다고 생각해요.
성격, 품성 personality

STEP 2　통문장 외우기

What do you think? Is that right?

Certainly. You're absolutely right about that.

I think you're mistaken about that.

What do you think of the new employee?

I think he has a very nice personality.

STEP 1 통문장 말하기

846 솔직한 의견을 주세요.
솔직한 honest

847 제가 어떻게 생각하는지 정말 알고 싶으세요?

848 물론 당신의 의견을 듣고 싶죠.
의견, 견해 opinion

849 우리 하와이로 휴가 가는 건 어때요?
우리 ~하는 건 어때요? Why don't we ~?

850 개인적으로 하와이보다 괌이 더 좋아요.
개인적인 의견을 말하면 personally

STEP 2 통문장 외우기

Please give me your honest opinion.

Do you really want to know what I think?

Of course I want to hear your opinions.

Why don't we go to Hawaii for our vacation?

Personally, I prefer Guam to Hawaii.

STEP 1 통문장 말하기

851 12월에는 하와이에 비가 올 것 같지 않나요?

852 우기인지 아닌지 모르겠네요.
우기 rainy season

853 왜 우리 브랜드 인지도가 낮죠? 뭐 아는 거 있어요?
(~에 대한) 인식, 관심 awareness

854 제 견해로는 우리는 소셜 미디어를 더 활용할 필요가 있어요.
~을 활용[이용]하다 make use of

855 그 의견은 받아들일 수 없어요. 시간과 자원이 들거든요.
자원, 재원 resources
소모하다 consume

STEP 2 통문장 외우기

Don't you think it's going to rain in Hawaii in December?

I don't know whether it is the rainy season or not.

Why is our brand awareness low? Do you have any idea?

In my opinion, we need to make more use of social media.

I can't accept that. It consumes time and resources.

STEP 3 패턴으로 훈련하기

❶ What do you think? Is that | right / wrong / correct / incorrect* | ?

*맞지 않는, 틀린

❷ | Certainly / Of course / That's for sure* | . You're absolutely right about that.

*확실하다, 분명하다

❸ What do you think of | the new employee / his opinion / my presentation | ?

❹ | I think / Personally, I think / In my opinion, / As far as I can tell* | he has a very nice personality.

*내가 알기로는

❺ Of course I want to hear your | opinions / thoughts / ideas | .

❻ | Why don't we go | to Hawaii for our vacation?
　　| How about going |

❼ Personally, I prefer | Guam | to | Hawaii | .
　　　　　　　　　　　| winter |　　| summer |
　　　　　　　　　　　| wine |　　　| beer |

❽ | Don't you think | it's going to rain in Hawaii in December?
　　| Do you think |
　　| Are you sure |

❾ I don't know whether | it is the rainy season | or not.
　　　　　　　　　　　　| John will leave today |
　　　　　　　　　　　　| she is coming |

❿ In my opinion, | we need to make more use of social media | .
　　　　　　　　　| it is just a matter of preference* |
　　　　　　　　　| you should hire* more staff |

기호, 선호/ 고용하다

STEP 4 대화로 훈련하기

A What do you think? Is that right?
B **① 물론이죠. 그 점에 대해선 당신이 전적으로 옳아요.**

A **② 그 점에 있어선 당신이 잘못 알고 있는 것 같네요.**
B We're not seeing eye to eye*.　　　　　　　　*의견이 일치하다

A **③ 신입 사원에 대해 어떻게 생각해요?**
B I think he has a very nice personality.

A That's a good idea. I like that.
B **④ 솔직한 의견을 주세요.**

A **⑤ 제가 어떻게 생각하는지 정말 알고 싶으세요?**
B Of course. Don't hold back*.　　　　　　　　*주저하다

A **⑥ 우리 하와이로 휴가 가는 건 어때요?**
B Personally, I prefer Guam to Hawaii.

A Isn't it the rainy season in Guam now?
B ❼ 우기인지 아닌지 모르겠네요.

A ❽ 왜 우리 브랜드 인지도가 낮죠? 뭐 아는 거 있어요?
B Not really. Let's take a survey.

A ❾ 제 견해로는 우리는 소셜 미디어를 더 활용할 필요가 있어요.
B Why haven't we thought of that before?

A What do you say to upgrading our Web site?
B ❿ 그 의견은 받아들일 수 없어요. 시간과 자원이 들거든요.

ANSWERS!!

1. Certainly. You're absolutely right about that.
2. I think you're mistaken about that.
3. What do you think of the new employee?
4. Please give me your honest opinion.
5. Do you really want to know what I think?
6. Why don't we go to Hawaii for our vacation?
7. I don't know whether it is the rainy season or not.
8. Why is our brand awareness low? Do you have any idea?
9. In my opinion, we need to make more use of social media.
10. I can't accept that. It consumes time and resources.

DAY 58 다양한 의견에 대응하기

STEP 1 통문장 말하기

856 당신의 의견을 알아야겠어요. 제게 동의하나요?
~에 동의하다 agree with

857 뭘 주장하고 싶은 거죠?
~을 주장하다 make a point

858 그건 진보적인 견해군요.
진보적인 liberal 견해, 관점 point of view

859 그는 좋은 아이디어가 많은 것 같아요.

860 모든 사람이 자신의 의견을 가질 권리가 있어요.
~에 대한 권리가 있다 be entitled to

STEP 2 통문장 외우기

I must know your opinion. Do you agree with me?

What point are you trying to make?

That's a liberal point of view.

He seems to have a lot of good ideas.

Everyone is entitled to his own opinion.

STEP 1 　통문장 말하기

861 모든 일에는 양면이 있어요.

862 당신은 당신 견해가 있고, 저는 제 견해가 있어요.

863 이 문제에 대해 우리는 서로 다른 의견을 가지고 있어요.
　　　　서로 다른, 대립하는 opposing

864 저와는 다른 방식으로 그것에 접근하는군요.
　　　　~에 접근하다[다가가다] approach

865 당신과 논쟁하지 않겠지만, 공정하지 못한 것 같은데요.
　　　　~와 언쟁을 벌이다 argue with　　공정하지 않은 unfair

There are two sides to everything.

You have your point of view, and I have mine.

We have opposing views on this.

You approach it in a different way than I do.

I won't argue with you, but I think you're being unfair.

STEP 1 통문장 말하기

866 그 문제를 더 논의해봤자 소용 없는 것 같아요.
더 further

867 말다툼을 시작할 의도는 아니었어요.
말다툼, 논쟁 argument   의도하다 mean

868 제게 어떤 대안들이 있나요?
대안 alternative

869 결국 우리의 관점이 그렇게 많이 다른 건 아니네요.
결국에는 after all   멀리 떨어진 far apart

870 우리는 의견 차를 좁힐 수 있을 거예요.
해소[해결]하다 resolve

STEP 2   통문장 외우기

I don't see any point in discussing the question further.

I didn't mean to start an argument.

What alternatives do I have?

Our views are not so far apart, after all.

We should be able to resolve our differences.

STEP 3 패턴으로 훈련하기

❶ I must know your opinion. **Do you agree with** me?
Do you disagree with
Are you for* or against*

*찬성하는/ *반대하는

❷ That's a **liberal** point of view.
conservative*
radical*

*보수적인
*급진적인

❸ Everyone **is entitled to** his own opinion.
has a right to*
deserves* the right to

*~을 요구할 권리가 있다
*~을 받을 만하다

❹ You have your **point of view**, and I have mine.
opinion
ideas

❺ We have **opposing** views on this.
conflicting*
totally* different

*상반되는
*완전히

❻ I won't argue with you, but I think you're being unfair / stubborn* / impractical* .

*고집스러운/*터무니없는

❼ I don't see any point in discussing / arguing / debating* the question further.

*토론[논쟁]하다

❽ I didn't mean / didn't want / wasn't trying to start an argument.

❾ Our views are not so far apart / totally different / close* together , after all.

*비슷한

❿ We should be able to resolve / settle / reconcile* our differences.

*일치하게 하다

STEP 4 대화로 훈련하기

A ① 당신의 의견을 알아야겠어요. 제게 동의하나요?
B I'm just not sure.

A Do you know what I mean?
B Not really. ② 뭘 주장하고 싶은 거죠?

A I think more tax breaks* should be given to the middle and lower classes.   *세금 우대, 감세
B ③ 그건 진보적인 견해군요.

A You've got it all wrong.
B Well, ④ 모든 사람이 자신의 의견을 가질 권리가 있어요.

A ⑤ 모든 일에는 양면이 있어요.
B I see what you're saying.

A I disagree with you.
B ⑥ 당신은 당신 견해가 있고, 저는 제 견해가 있어요.

A **저와는 다른 방식으로 그것에 접근하는군요.**
B Then speak your mind.

A I think women shouldn't serve in the army.
B **당신과 논쟁하지 않겠지만, 공정하지 못한 것 같은데요.**

A I don't see any point in discussing the question further.
B I'm sorry. **말다툼을 시작할 의도는 아니었어요.**

A Forget it. We're wasting our time.
B No, **결국 우리의 관점이 그렇게 많이 다른 건 아니네요.**

ANSWERS!!

1 I must know your opinion. Do you agree with me? 2 What point are you trying to make?
3 That's a liberal point of view. 4 everyone is entitled to his own opinion.
5 There are two sides to everything. 6 You have your point of view, and I have mine.
7 You approach it in a different way than I do.
8 I won't argue with you, but I think you're being unfair.
9 I didn't mean to start an argument. 10 our views are not so far apart, after all.

DAY 59 조언과 충고

STEP 1 통문장 말하기

871 당신에게 조언을 좀 할게요.
조언, 충고 advice

872 그게 마음에 들지 않는다면 뭔가 말해주세요.

873 제 조언을 원한다면 당신은 가지 않는 게 좋을 것 같아요.

874 저도 알아서 결정할 나이가 되었어요.
결심하다, 결정하다 make up one's (own) mind

875 제 생각으로는 당신은 오늘 밤 집에 있어야 할 것 같아요.
~해야 하다 ought to

목표는 단 하나.
1초의 주저함도 없이
자동으로 튀어나오게 하라!

STEP 2 통문장 외우기

Let me give you a little advice.

If you don't like it, please say something.

If you want my advice, I don't think you should go.

I'm old enough to make up my own mind.

My feeling is that you ought to stay home tonight.

STEP 1 통문장 말하기

876 제 조언을 받아들이지 않는다면 후회할 거예요.
후회하다 be sorry

877 제가 상관할 바는 아니지만 당신은 일을 더 열심히 해야 할 것 같아요.
~가 상관할 일이 아니다 none of one's business

878 화내지 마세요. 제 생각을 말하고 싶었을 뿐이에요.
화내다 take offense

879 제 견해로는 그 집은 그들이 부르는 값만큼의 가치가 없는 것 같아요.

880 충고는 감사하지만 이건 제 스스로 해결해야 하는 거예요.
이해하다, 알아내다 figure out

STEP 2 통문장 외우기

If you don't take my advice, you'll be sorry.

It's none of my business, but I think you should work harder.

Please don't take offense. I only wanted to tell you what I think.

In my opinion, the house isn't worth the price they're asking.

Thanks for the advice, but this is something I have to figure out myself.

STEP 1   통문장 말하기

881 그 일에 대해선 잊고 처음부터 다시 시작했으면 해요.
일, 사건 incident   처음부터 다시 시작하다 start over again

882 그냥 제안일 뿐이니 당신 좋을 대로 하면 돼요.
제안 suggestion

883 늘 당신 일에 간섭하지 않으려고 애써왔어요.
문제 affair   간섭하다, 개입하다 interfere

884 대체로 그의 반응은 호의적이에요.
보통, 대개 in general   호의적인 favorable

885 그는 누구의 말도 들으려 하지 않아요.
말해봐야 당신 입만 아파요.
말해봐야 소용없다 waste one's breath

STEP 2 통문장 외우기

I suggest that you forget about the incident and start over again.

It's only a suggestion, and you can do what you please.

I've always tried not to interfere in your affairs.

In general, his reactions have been favorable.

He won't listen to anybody. You're just wasting your breath.

STEP 3 패턴으로 훈련하기

❶ If you [don't like it / are not happy with it / don't agree with me], please say something.

❷ If [you want / you care for / you're interested in] my advice, I don't think you should go.

❸ I'm [old / grown up / smart*] enough to make up my own mind.

*똑똑한, 영리한

❹ My feeling is that you [ought to / should / had better] stay home tonight.

❺ If you don't take my advice, you'll [be sorry / regret* it later / be in trouble*].

*후회하다
*곤경에 빠지다

6. It's [none of my business / not my place to say], but I think you should work harder.

7. Please don't [take offense / get upset* / take it that way*].

    *속상한
    *그런 식으로 받아들이다

8. [In my opinion / As I see it / As far as I can tell], the house isn't worth the price they're asking.

9. Thanks for the advice, but this is something I have to [figure out myself / work out myself / decide alone].

10. In general, his reactions have been [favorable / positive* / negative*].

    *긍정적인
    *부정적인

STEP 4   대화로 훈련하기

A ① 당신에게 조언을 좀 할게요.
B   What are you trying to say?

A ② 그게 마음에 들지 않는다면 뭔가 말해주세요.
B   It's fine. Thanks for your advice.

A   Do you think I should go to graduate school?
B ③ 제 조언을 원한다면 당신은 가지 않는 게 좋을 것 같아요.

A   Don't go out with Mike.
B ④ 저도 알아서 결정할 나이가 되었어요.

A ⑤ 제 조언을 받아들이지 않는다면 후회할 거예요.
B   Get off my case!* I'll do it when I do it.   *내 일에 상관하지 말아요!

A   I've been demoted* at work.   *강등되다
B ⑥ 제가 상관할 바는 아니지만 당신은 일을 더 열심히 해야 할 것 같아요.

A **화내지 마세요. 제 생각을 말하고 싶었을 뿐이에요.**
B That's it? I'm fine, don't worry.

A **그 일에 대해선 잊고 처음부터 다시 시작했으면 해요.**
B Thanks! It's so sweet of you to say that.

A Lisa and I are in a serious relationship.
B **늘 당신 일에 간섭하지 않으려고 애써왔어요,** but you can't see what she's really like.

A I kept telling him to quit smoking, but he didn't take my advice.
B **그는 누구의 말도 들으려 하지 않아요. 말해봐야 당신 입만 아파요.**

ANSWERS!!

1 Let me give you a little advice.   2 If you don't like it, please say something.
3 If you want my advice, I don't think you should go.
4 I'm old enough to make up my own mind.   5 If you don't take my advice, you'll be sorry.
6 It's none of my business, but I think you should work harder.
7 Please don't take offense. I only wanted to tell you what I think.
8 I suggest that you forget about the incident and start over again.
9 I've always tried not to interfere in your affairs,
10 He won't listen to anybody. You're just wasting your breath.

DAY 60 의사 결정

STEP 1 통문장 말하기

886 어떻게 하기로 결정했어요?

887 당신의 결정이 무엇인지 무척 알고 싶어요.
~하기를 열망하다 be anxious to

888 캘리포니아에 가기로 확실히 결정했어요.
확실히, 분명히 definitely

889 우린 당신의 결정을 기꺼이 받아들이겠어요.
기꺼이 ~하다 be willing to

890 당신이 옳은 선택을 했다고 확신해요.
확신하는 confident

STEP 2 통문장 외우기

What have you decided?

I'm anxious to know what your decision is.

I've definitely decided to go to California.

We're willing to accept your decision.

I'm confident you've made the right choice.

STEP 1 통문장 말하기

891 당신이 마음을 바꾸도록 설득하고 싶어요.
설득하다 persuade

892 제 조언을 받아들이시겠어요?

893 잘 생각해본 후 결정한 사항을 제게 알려주세요.
~을 심사숙고하다 think over

894 그는 새 차를 사지 않기로 결정한 것 같네요.
~하지 않기로 결정하다 decide against   추측하다 assume

895 그의 결정에 영향을 줄 만한 어떤 말도 하고 싶지 않았어요.
영향을 주다[미치다] influence

STEP 2 통문장 외우기

I want to persuade you to change your mind.

Will you accept my advice?

After you think it over, please let me know what you decide.

I assume he's decided against buying a new car.

I didn't want to say anything to influence his decision.

STEP 1 통문장 말하기

896 그가 결심을 하기까지 오랜 시간이 걸렸어요.

897 모든 사실을 다 알지 못한 채 결정을 내리긴 어렵죠.
결정하다 make a decision

898 회사에서 더 좋은 조건을 제안했지만, 애나는 일을 그만두기로 결정했어요.
제안하다, 권하다 offer
그만두다 quit

899 그녀는 그것이 자신에게 아무런 영향을 주지 않는다고 주장해요.
영향을 주다, 차이를 낳다 make a difference

900 그녀는 마음을 바꾸지 않으려 해요.
거절[거부]하다 refuse

STEP 2 통문장 외우기

It took him a long time to make up his mind.

It's difficult to make a decision without knowing all the facts.

The company offered better conditions, but Anna's decided to quit her job.

She insists that it doesn't make any difference to her.

She refuses to change her mind.

STEP 3 패턴으로 훈련하기

❶ I'm [anxious / curious*] to know what your decision is.

*궁금한

❷ I've [definitely / almost / halfway*] decided to go to California.

*부분적으로, 불완전하게

❸ We're willing to [accept / follow* / agree to] your decision.

*따르다

❹ I'm [confident / sure / certain] you've made the right choice.

❺ I want to [persuade / ask / urge*] you to change your mind.

*촉구하다

⑥ Will you accept my [advice / decision / proposal*]?

*제안, 제의

⑦ I assume he's decided against [buying a new car / going to the movies / getting married this year].

⑧ I didn't want to say anything to [influence / affect / complicate*] his decision.

*복잡하게 만들다

⑨ She insists that it doesn't [make any difference / matter / mean anything] to her.

⑩ She [refuses to / doesn't want to / isn't willing to] change her mind.

STEP 4 대화로 훈련하기

A ① 어떻게 하기로 결정했어요?
B I've decided to buy the new Toyota hybrid car.

A Where have you decided to go this summer?
B ② 캘리포니아에 가기로 확실히 결정했어요.

A We are relocating* both of you to San Francisco. *전근 보내다
B ③ 우린 당신의 결정을 기꺼이 받아들이겠어요.

A ④ 당신이 옳은 선택을 했다고 확신해요.
B Thanks for trusting me.

A I'm switching departments.
B ⑤ 당신이 마음을 바꾸도록 설득하고 싶어요.

A Please accept my resignation.
B ⑥ 잘 생각해본 후 결정한 사항을 제게 알려주세요.

A Why didn't you stop him from resigning?
B ❼ 그의 결정에 영향을 줄 만한 어떤 말도 하고 싶지 않았어요.

A ❽ 그가 결심을 하기까지 오랜 시간이 걸렸어요.
B It's difficult to make a decision without knowing all the facts.

A ❾ 회사에서 더 좋은 조건을 제안했지만, 애나는 일을 그만두기로 결정했어요.
B Things won't be the same without her.

A Did you ask her to reconsider?
B Of course, but ❿ 그녀는 마음을 바꾸지 않으려 해요.

ANSWERS!!

1 What have you decided? 2 I've definitely decided to go to California.
3 We're willing to accept your decision. 4 I'm confident you've made the right choice.
5 I want to persuade you to change your mind.
6 After you think it over, please let me know what you decide.
7 I didn't want to say anything to influence his decision.
8 It took him a long time to make up his mind.
9 The company offered better conditions, but Anna's decided to quit her job.
10 she refuses to change her mind.

**You Did
A Very Good Job**